SPOTT'S
CANINE MISCELLANY

SPOTT'S
CANINE MISCELLANY

By Mike Darton

ABRAMS IMAGE, NEW YORK

Creative Director *Peter Bridgewater*
Publisher *Jason Hook*
Editorial Director *Caroline Earle*
Senior Editor *Lorraine Turner*
Art Director *Clare Harris*
Designer *Richard Constable*
Illustrations *Ivan Hissey, Joanna Kerr, Tony Walter-Bellue & other old dogs*

Library of Congress Cataloging-in-Publication Data

Darton, Mike.
Spott's canine miscellany / by Mike Darton.
p. cm.
ISBN 978-0-8109-2124-5 (harry n. abrams, inc.)
1. Dogs—Miscellanea. I. Title.
SF426.2.D37 2009
636.7—dc22
2008038303

This book was created by **Ivy Press**

Printed and bound in China
10 9 8 7 6 5 4 3 2 1
Abrams Image books are available at special discounts when purchased in quantity
for premiums and promotions as well as fundraising or educational use. Special editions
can also be created to specification. For details, contact specialmarkets@hnabooks.com
or the address below.

HNA
harry n. abrams, inc.
a subsidiary of La Martinière Groupe

115 West 18th Street
New York, NY 10011
www.hnabooks.com

*"Outside of a dog, a book is man's best friend.
Inside a dog, it's too dark to read "*

GROUCHO MARX

THE DOG FAMILY

The family Canidae includes dogs, jackals, and foxes and currently comprises 13 genera and 37 recognized species, as classified below:

CANIDAE

The genus *Canis*

Gray wolf *C. lupus*
Red wolf *C. rufus*
Golden jackal *C. aureus*
Simien jackal *C. simensis*
Silver-backed jackal
C. meso-melas
Side-striped jackal *C. adustus*
Coyote *C. latrans*
Domestic dog *C. familiaris*
Dingo *C. dingo*—but in reality
the dingo is simply a domestic dog
that has reverted to a feral state

The genus *Vulpes*

Red fox *V. vulpes*
Gray fox *V. cinereoargenteus*
Island gray fox *V. littoralis*
Fennec fox *V. zerda*
Rüppell's fox *V. ruppelli*
Indian fox *V. bengalensis*
Blanford's fox *V. cana*
Swift fox *V. velox*
Cape fox *V. chama*
Corsac fox *V. corsac*
Pale fox *V. pallida*
Kit fox *V. macrotis*
Tibetan sand fox *V. ferrilata*

The genus *Dusicyon*

Colpeo fox *D. culpaeus*
Pampas fox *D. gymnocercus*
Chilla or South American fox
D. griseus
Small-eared fox *D. microtis*
Sechura fox *D. sechurae*
Hoary fox *D. vetulus*

Other genera

Raccoon dog
Nyctereutes procyonoides★
Bush dog *Speothos venaticus*
Small-eared dog *Atelocynus microtis*
African wild dog *Lycaon pictus*
Dhole *Cuon alpinus*★
Maned wolf *Chrysocyon*★ *brachyurus*
Arctic fox *Alopex lagopus*
Bat-eared fox *Otocyon*★ *megalotis*
Crab-eating fox *Cerdocyon*★ *thous*

★ In the Latin names of the "other genera," the element *cuon* or *cyon* represents the ancient Greek *kuōn*, "dog."

THE DOG'S SENSE OF TASTE

Dogs have fewer taste buds than humans—probably 1,700–2,000 altogether, compared with humans' 9,000—which is why humans (with some exceptions) tend to be much more choosy about what they eat and why dogs in general distinguish only between what they like and what they find disgusting. Indeed, dogs are said to have 6 times less taste discrimination than humans, but to make up for that (and more), they use their phenomenal sense of smell in combination with taste. (Even in humans, taste is believed to be fundamentally involved with smell.)

THE SYMBOLIC DOG

In statuary, and particularly on monuments and tombs, the dog may be placed at the feet of a woman to symbolize her affection, loyalty, and fidelity—just as a lion is placed at the feet of a man to signify his courage and magnanimity. The medieval Crusaders were often represented on their sarcophagi with their feet resting on a dog, in order to show that they followed the Christian precepts of the Lord as faithfully as a dog follows at the heels of his master.

THE TALBOT: AN EXTINCT BREED

Among the list of 21 famous dog breeds that over the centuries have for one reason or another become extinct is the Talbot. The Talbot was an enormous hunting dog brought by the Norman conquerors to England in 1066, where it became popular for the grand hunts of stags in the forested parks of aristocrats. This popularity continued until at least 1500, by which time the dog had been given the name of the lordly English Talbot family, who were famous for keeping such animals. But the dogs required vast quantities of food and constant care, and as those hunts gradually ceased, so the dogs died out. Always depicted with a protruding tongue, the dog's picture is among the heraldic devices on the coat of arms of the town of Sudbury, in Suffolk, England. A Talbot is additionally the mascot for the school district of Hampton Township, in western Pennsylvania.

THURBER ON CANINE WISDOM

"The dog has seldom been successful in pulling man up to its level of sagacity, but man has frequently dragged the dog down to his."
JAMES THURBER (1894–1961) *U.S. humorist*

ASSEMBLING A DOG

The following parts are required:

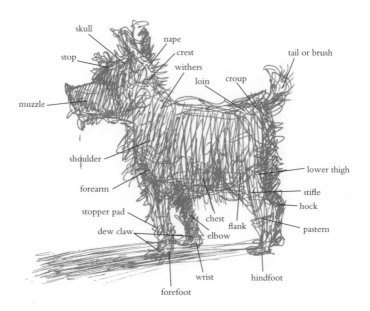

T HE CROUP—the hinder top part of the trunk of the body—is an English word derived through Norman French from Old Germanic, and in a horse is where the pillion passenger or assistant huntsman would sit behind the hunter, handing him his weapons as and when required. He was thus known as the croupier, and this is why the present-day croupier now hands out the cards, chips, and markers as and when required to the gamblers at a casino.

SHORT-TERM MEMORY

Except when trained or specifically taught something by repetition, dogs have a comparatively short-term casual memory. Research suggests that in ordinary circumstances a dog remembers something for only 5 minutes (whereas a cat can remember for up to 16 hours or until the next lengthy sleep, whichever happens to be the shorter time).

RIN TIN TIN

R IN TIN TIN was originally (in the form Rintintin) the name of the "male" half of a pair of brightly colored dolls made out of yarn by young French women and given as good-luck charms to young men going off to fight in the trenches of World War I. When U.S. soldiers joined the fray in northern Europe, many of them received similar attentions from French demoiselles, and once the war was over, the yarn dolls—with the notion of associated good luck in a combat setting—returned with the soldiers to the other side of the Atlantic. Very soon thereafter, stories of the dog Rin Tin Tin and his United States Army "family" became current. The first Rin Tin Tin movie was made in 1922. The final Rin Tin Tin television series ended in 1959, although blood descendants of the original canine actor still make charity guest appearances under the Rin Tin Tin name.

REASONS FOR TRIMMING A POODLE

The original idea behind trimming a poodle as if it were a topiarized hedge was to shave the dog's profusely thick coat to increase its agility—specifically to enable it to swim better through rivers and across lakes—while out hunting with its medieval aristocratic European owner. The "cuffs" around the ankles and hips were left to protect against arthritis/rheumatism in the cold and draughty mansion or castle in which it was kenneled.

THE IDITAROD RACE

The annual Iditarod dog-sledding race in Alaska is now a celebrated international event, but by media tradition it commemorates an emergency dash in 1925 over 1,049 miles (1,688 kilometers) of the existing (longer) Iditarod Trail by 25 teams of "mushers" transporting medicine from Anchorage to treat an epidemic of diphtheria in Nome. "Iditarod" is a version of the Chinook word *haiditarod*, "remote [area]."

The first race over the current (shorter) course was in 1973; the winner did it in 20 days and 1 hour. In 2002, the winning time was just 8 days and 23 hours. Two women have won the event 5 times (1985–1988 and 1990). The narrowest winning margin so far is 1 second, in 1978.

DOG BEQUESTS

It is estimated that about 1 million dogs in the United States are the primary beneficiaries of their owner's will.

DO DOGS LAUGH?

HYENAS ARE SAID TO LAUGH—but then, despite the way they look, hyenas belong to their own family and are not of the family Canidae. However, research and careful analysis in 2001 revealed that dogs in play may pant in a special way (involving a slightly more breathy exhalation) that seems to have an effect on other dogs that motivates or inspires them toward further playfulness. This is not exactly what most humans might think of as laughter, but it was described as such by Patricia Simonet of Sierra Nevada College.

Dogs quite often *look* as though they are laughing. But does facial expression count? Most dogs can assume any of more than 90 facial expressions that are understood by other dogs. Sadly, some domesticated types of dog—notably the bulldog and pit bull terrier, if "domesticated" is the right word for these—have had most facial expressions bred out of them. They may consequently find themselves having to fight their way out of trouble with other dogs simply because they fail to exhibit the appropriate expression of passive disinterest at the vital moment.

AESOP'S FABLE: THE BELLED DOG

A dog kept at home earned such a reputation for biting visitors that his master put a bell around his neck to warn everybody of the dog's approach. Far from understanding that purpose, however, the dog believed that he had been given some sort of award or badge of merit, and went around showing off his mark of distinction to all of the other animals in the household. His pride was cut short only when one old hound told him, quietly and dispassionately, that the bell was effectively a symbol of disgrace, and that he really must learn to distinguish notoriety from fame.

KUNDERA ON DOGS & HEAVEN

"Dogs are our link to paradise. They don't know evil or jealousy or discontent. To sit with a dog on a hillside on a glorious afternoon is to be back in Eden, where doing nothing was not boring—it was peace."
MILAN KUNDERA (b. 1929) *Czech-born French author and political critic*

THE YAWNING POOCH

When a dog yawns, it is most often an expression of contentment instead of one that signifies tiredness or boredom.

PUPS PER LITTER

The number of pups per litter varies both according to the breed of the parents and their respective conditions of health. The figures below are therefore (inevitably) statistical averages only. But for each breed named, the average number of pups per litter (according to a reputable source) is:

Pekingese	10.0	Norwegian elkhound	6.0
Large dachshund	8.7	Springer spaniel	6.0
Saint Bernard	8.5	Siberian husky	5.9
Golden retriever	8.1	Bulldog	5.9
German shepherd	8.0	French bulldog	5.8
Collie	7.9	Dalmatian	5.8
Labrador	7.8	Bernese mountain dog	5.8
Mastiff	7.7	Bedlington terrier	5.6
Airedale terrier	7.6	Welsh corgi	5.5
Basenji	7.6	Dandie Dinmont terrier	5.3
Doberman(n) pinscher	7.6	Standard schnauzer	5.1
Rottweiler	7.5	Australian terrier	5.0
Gordon setter	7.5	Papillon	5.0
Irish setter	7.2	Boxer	5.0
Greyhound	6.8	Scottish terrier (Scottie dog)	4.9
Pointer	6.7	Black Norwegian elkhound	4.8
Small poodle	6.4	Lapland reindeer dog	4.8
English setter	6.3	Cocker spaniel	4.8
English foxhound	6.3	Manchester terrier	4.7
Samoyed	6.0	Kerry blue terrier	4.7

ROOSEVELT'S DOGS AT THE WHITE HOUSE

THE ROOSEVELT MEMORIAL in Washington, D.C. features a bronze of Franklin D.'s best-known doggy companion, a Scottish terrier (Scottie dog) called Fala (1940–1952). During Roosevelt's presidency, he actually owned at least 10 other dogs, one of whom, Major, achieved a different sort of personal celebrity when—to the horror of all present—he attacked the pants of the visiting British Prime Minister, Ramsay MacDonald.

FRANKLIN JONES ON WASHING A DOG

"Anybody who doesn't know what soap tastes like never washed a dog."
FRANKLIN P. JONES (1853–1935) *U.S. humorist and writer of aphorisms*

DOG SOUP

A lot of people find plain water unpleasant to drink, unless they are particularly hot and thirsty. Maybe that's why one Australian expression for water is "dog's soup" (although it should be noted that the expression was transported to Australia with the convicts from nineteenth-century London, England).

Even less appetizing to more people, however, is *poshintang*, or *bosintang* (said by ill-wishers to literally mean "preserved corpse stew"), also known as *gaejang*, which is a soup made with genuine dog meat. In Korea, where it is a popular summertime dish, consumption of this soup is said to be highly beneficial to human health and vitality.

CANINE EYESIGHT

Dogs have better low-light vision than humans, thanks to a special mirrorlike coating behind the retina that reflects back onto the retina light that has already passed through it. The mirrorlike surface is known as the "tapetum" and is the source of the "eyeshine"—the yellow, green, or even red light that may be seen in a dog's eyes when the dog looks straight at you from a darker area, or in photos taken using flash photography. But color vision in a dog is less discriminatory than color vision in most humans; dogs effectively have the equivalent of human red-green color blindness (dichromatism).

Nonetheless, dogs have wide vision in relation to the diameter of the eyeball because of a special horizontal line or "streak" of light-sensitive cells across the retina that adds detail to peripheral vision. Moreover, the eyes of some dogs are set in the skull so as to give them a more than 180-degree visual range.

BASIC COMMANDS

Sign seen hanging on the door of a vet/dog therapist's office:

Gone to get a sandwich
Back in 5 minutes
SIT! STAY!

THE GREAT DOG IN THE SKY

It was probably the ancient Egyptians who first associated the bright star we call Sirius with a dog—although to them the dog in question was actually the jackal-headed god Anubis, guide of dead souls to the Underworld and assistant to the great Lord of the Underworld, Osiris. The Egyptians called the star Set or Sutek, and because it was one of the 3 Morning Stars visible during the year, they regarded it also as a manifestation of the goddess Isis, the sister and consort of Osiris. When the ancient Greeks eventually conquered Egypt, they adapted the mythology they found there. The "dog" Set became *seirios kuōn*, "the scorching dog," and from that time onward was regarded as the brightest star in a whole constellation known as The Dog. The myth grew that this particular dog was the hunting companion of Orion (Actaeon) and was in pursuit of the Great Bear or of various other stellar game animals.

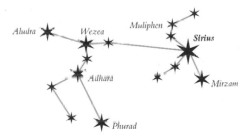

In due course, the Romans added to these notions in several ways. First they insisted that The Dog itself had a companion constellation, and named the original Canis Major and the new, smaller set of stars Canis Minor. Then they perceived yet more dogs in the heavens—the hunting dogs (*Canes venatici*) of Boötes. The name of the brightest star in Canis Major was adapted to Sirius.

The current names of all the other named stars in the constellation come to us through medieval Arabic.

CANINE CUPID

Renowned poet Elizabeth Barrett's dog was dognapped and held for ransom—a not rare occurrence in London, England, in 1845. Elizabeth's father, who she greatly feared, refused to pay the 6 guinea ransom, which led her to overcome her terror of him, seeking the help of family acquaintance Robert Browning. Together they recovered the dog. Thereafter she felt confident enough to elope with Robert, becoming Mrs. Barrett Browning, and she went to live in happy comfort in Italy. And the dog went too.

TOP DOGS IN THE U.S. & U.K.

Most popular dog breeds since 2007:

IN THE U.S.	IN THE U.K.
1. . . . . *Labrador*	1. . . . . *Labrador*
2. . . . . *Yorkshire terrier*	2. . . . . *Cocker spaniel*
3. . . . . *German shepherd*	3. . . . . *English springer spaniel*
4. . . . .*Golden retriever*	4. . . . . *Staffordshire bull terrier*
5. . . . . *Beagle*	5. . . . . *German shepherd*
6. . . . . *Boxer*	6. . . . . . .*Cavalier King Charles spaniel*
7. . . . . *Dachshund*	7. . . . . *Golden retriever*
8. . . . . *Poodle*	8. . . . . *Border terrier*
9. . . . . *Shih Tzu*	9. . . . . *West Highland terrier*
10. . . . . *Bulldog*	10. . . . . *Boxer*

THE ALAUNT: AN EXTINCT BREED

Among the list of 21 famous dog breeds that over the centuries have become extinct is the Alaunt. The Alaunt was a short-haired working dog not unlike a bulldog, bred in an area from what is now southern Russia to Iran in the fourth and fifth centuries CE.

PATRON SAINT OF DOGS

The patron saint of dogs and dog lovers is St. Roch (or Rochus, Roque, Rock, Rocco), who was born *c.* 1295 (or *c.* 1350) in Montpellier, France, into an aristocratic family. He renounced his heritage to become a peripatetic minister to plague victims. In Rome, Italy, he caught the plague himself and retreated to seclusion in a forest near Piacenza, where he was at times visited by other plague sufferers, whom he is reputed to have healed. A dog brought him food daily and licked his sores until he recovered. Thereafter, according to one authority, he went back to his aristocratic home, found all but one of his relatives (an uncle) had died, and was cast into prison (with the dog) for "impersonating" who he really was (since the uncle coveted his inheritance). Another authority suggests (with better provenance) that St. Roch was incarcerated as a spy in Lombardy, Italy.

Either way, while in prison he cared for other inmates until he died, aged 32, in 1327 (or *c.* 1382). Miracles were acclaimed at his tomb soon afterward. He is thus also the patron saint of sufferers from epidemics, knee and skin problems, and of invalids in general. His feast day is August 16.

TELEPHONE MESSAGES

One third of all U.S. dog owners admit to leaving telephone messages for their dog on their answering machines or to actually talking to their dog over the phone.

SENSE OF HEARING

The average dog has a hearing range of about 67 Hz to 45,000 Hz—whereas an adult human on average has a maximum range of about 64 Hz to 23,000 Hz, the higher frequencies greatly diminishing with age down to maybe 8,000 Hz. (The average cat is said to have a hearing range of about 55 Hz to 62,000 Hz, but compare that to the bat's extraordinary range of 2,000 Hz to 110,000 Hz.)

The directional sense of their hearing is increased for dogs by the shape of their ears, the ability to turn their ears (using a combination of at least 18 different muscles per ear) to pinpoint a source, and by extra perception of pitch and tone. This means that dogs can normally hear and pinpoint the source of a sound at about 4 times the maximum distance that an adult human can. On the other hand, absolute silence makes a dog nervous.

LASSIE

THE BORDER COLLIE LASSIE first appeared in the short story "Lassie Come Home" by Eric Mowbray Knight, published in the *Saturday Evening Post* in 1938 and extended as a novel that was issued in 1940. The basis for the work was apparently Knight's real-life collie, Toots. Three years later, the movie of the book (called *Lassie Come Home*) starred Elizabeth Taylor and Roddy McDowall, and it was such a success it generated two more movies (*Son of Lassie*, 1945; *Courage of Lassie*, 1946) and a radio series (1946–49). The subsequent U.S. TV series ran from 1954 to 1973. In the 588 episodes of the TV show, all 6 dogs who consecutively played the eponymous female role were in fact male, mainly because they had to seem large in comparison to the lead child actor who would inevitably grow as time went on—notably with Tommy Rettig as Jeff Miller, 1954–57, and Jon Provost as Timmy Martin, 1957–64. Further TV series were produced by different TV companies during the 1980s and 1990s. A remake of the original film (this time produced in the U.K. and starring Peter O'Toole and Samantha Morton) was released in 2006.

CANINE GENES & BODY SIZE

The total number of genes in dogs is still under scientific debate, but the number currently assumed is 100,000—compared with between 20,000 and 25,000 for humans (which is astonishingly low). However, similarity between DNA sequences in humans and in dogs is already officially "over 85 percent" and is likely, when the canine genome is fully extrapolated, to be more than 90 percent. Meanwhile, DNA identicality explains why dogs nonetheless have the largest variation in body size of any land animal and yet remain dogs: only one small segment of genetic material tends to control body size, a regulatory sequence on dog chromosome 15, associated with a gene that is known to influence the presence and activity in the body of a growth hormone.

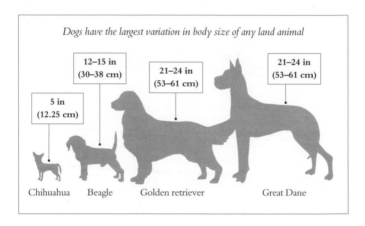

Dogs have the largest variation in body size of any land animal

5 in (12.25 cm) — Chihuahua

12–15 in (30–38 cm) — Beagle

21–24 in (53–61 cm) — Golden retriever

21–24 in (53–61 cm) — Great Dane

AESOP'S FABLE: THE FARM DOGS

A truly terrible storm keeps a farmer penned tightly within his farm day after day. Time goes steadily by but still the farmer is unable to get away as the wind howls and the rains lash down. All too soon he has to kill his few sheep to eat, and then his goats. Later still, as the storm enters its third month, he has to slaughter his oxen just to stay alive. But at that the dogs of the farm decide to run away—for "He who mistreats his own family is not to be trusted as a friend."

—— THE AMBROSE BIERCE DEFINITION OF DOG ——

"Dog: A kind of additional or subsidiary Deity designed
to catch the overflow and surplus of the world's worship."

AMBROSE BIERCE (1842–1914) *U.S. journalist and satirist*

—————————— CAVE CANEM ——————————

Everyone knows that *cave canem* is the Latin for "Beware of the dog."
Except it isn't. Not exactly, anyway. It is much more legal and officious
than that. The words are found many times on the house walls and gateposts of
ancient Rome and other Roman cities—notably Pompeii and Herculaneum—
and are not so much a warning as a disclaimer. The verb *cavere* in Latin
(which is generally translated as "to beware," "to watch out for," or "to be
on one's guard against") was in fact a technical legal term. If a passerby had
had ample opportunity to read the notice and had nonetheless been bitten by
the dog, the fact that prior warning had been posted in these words meant
that there was no question that legal action for injury or compensation against
the dog's owner could not be taken. Readers of the notice went further
on their way at their own risk.

The modern Italian for "Beware of the dog" is *Attenti al cane*.

—————————— DOGS & TEMPERATURE ——————————

Dogs are more reactive to high
temperatures than humans. They
rely on breathing rapidly (panting)
to exhale hot air and inhale cool,
but if the air temperature is already
hot—and especially if it is close to
body temperature—panting may
not be efficient enough. This might
particularly be the case if the dog
is bred for shortness and squatness
of face or is left in a confined space
with a muzzle on. Moreover, dogs
sweat only through the pads of their
feet. The result may all too quickly
be heat stroke, which requires early
diagnosis and immediate treatment
by a medical practitioner.

—————————— THE DOG AS DOMINATOR ——————————

In light of the fact that dogs have less of a sense of taste than humans, it is
often said that dogs who are conspicuously choosy about their food are not so
much canine gourmets but more the types of dog who enjoy manipulating/
demonstrating their power over their owner.

A DOG'S LIFE IN THE WHITE HOUSE

BARBARA BUSH, wife of President Bush the elder, wrote a book about her springer spaniel, Millie (*Millie's Book: As Dictated to Barbara Bush*, Harper Perennial, 1992). Purporting to give the inside story of life at the White House from the dog's viewpoint, it was popular enough to remain on the bestseller list for 5 months (or 7 months, according to some).

MAN'S BEST FRIEND

It is surely not only in English that the dog is often described as "man's best friend." Yet the use of that phrase had to start somewhere—and a good case for its beginning might be found in 1870 in Missouri.

It was a good case, too—in the Court of Appeals of that state— made by one Senator George Graham Vest on behalf of his client, a Mr. Burden, who was claiming compensatory damages following the quite possibly accidental shooting of his dog by a determinedly unapologetic neighbor, Mr. Hornsby. The case had already been through various lesser courts without Mr. Burden receiving any satisfaction whatsoever. But this time

was different—this time Senator Vest decided to base his argument less on facts and more on trying to sway the emotions of the jury. He launched into a fervent and effusive paean of praise to the overall loyalty, companionship, and persistent good nature of family dogs. He may or may not actually have used the expression "man's best friend," but those words were certainly used in the extraordinarily lengthy coverage of his speech in the local, and then the national, press.

And in the courtroom the jurors were so overwhelmed that they insisted on awarding Mr. Burden more than twice the damages for which he had sued Mr. Hornsby.

POPULAR DOG NAMES

Popular names for dogs are often names that might otherwise have been imposed upon human infants. However, a survey in the United Kingdom at the turn of the millennium outlined popular *categories* of names for dogs, which included:

Brands	*e.g., Levi, Gucci*
Celebrities	*e.g., Jordan, Kylie, Britney*
Sports stars	*e.g., Beckham, Rooney, Rio*
Fictional heroes	*e.g., Merlin, Frodo, Indiana*
Alcoholic drinks	*e.g., Brandy, Sherry, Whisky*
Food	*e.g., Chips, Pumpkin, Noodle*
Confectionery	*e.g., Rolo, Twix, Fudge*

DOG-OWNING HOUSEHOLDS

Since 2002:

IN THE U.K.
✳ Almost 1 in 2 households has at least 1 dog
✳ Which corresponds to about 10.2 dogs per 100 residents of the country (as opposed to 12.5 cats per 100 residents of the country)
✳ And 21 percent of dog-owning households have more than 1 dog (although there are 20 percent more cat-owning households overall).

IN AUSTRALIA
✳ 38 percent of households have at least 1 dog
✳ Which corresponds to about 19.5 dogs per 100 residents of the country
✳ And 43 percent of dog-owning households have more than 1 dog.

IN CANADA
✳ 27 percent of households have at least 1 dog
✳ Which equates to about 17 dogs per 100 residents in Canada
✳ And more than 60 percent of dog-owning households have more than 1 dog.

PRAIRIE DOGS

Just as polecats and meerkats are not cats, dormice are not mice, and clothes horses are not horses, prairie dogs are not dogs at all. They are a genus (*Cynomys*) of burrowing grassland rodents rather like miniature woodchucks. And indeed, their being named partly after their grassland habitat may correspond to the first use of the word "prairie" in English—a word derived via the French explorers of what is now the northeastern United States ultimately from the Latin *prataria*, "grassy place." But the creatures are called dogs because of the high-pitched barking sounds they make, and the fact that those sounds together comprise a code that is a recognizable system of communication. Incidentally, the generic name *Cynomys* means "dog-mouse."

FINAL FAREWELL

• MAJOR •

Born a dog, Died a gentleman

Epitaph on a dog's gravestone in Maryland

———— BENCHLEY ON THE DOG AS TEACHER ————

"A dog teaches a boy fidelity, perseverance,
and to turn around 3 times before lying down."
ROBERT BENCHLEY (1889–1945) *U.S. humorous journalist and actor*

———— THE CANARY ISLANDS, PLACE OF DOGS ————

The Canary Islands—the group of volcanic islands some 60 miles (100 kilometers) west of the coast of Morocco in northwest Africa—were named not after the birds now known as canaries but after the wild dogs that overran the islands during the first century BCE. The Romans were hoping to explore the ocean to the west as they had been doing for some decades along the coasts both north and south of the Strait of Gibraltar. Geographers duly sought the advice of one Iuba, a Rome-educated son of a ruler of a north African kingdom, whose description of the outlying archipelago caused the Roman author Pliny to call the group *Canaria* ("place of dogs," from *canes,* "dogs.")

———— THE FIRST DOG IN SPACE ————

LAIKA, a mongrel stray, on November 3, 1957, became the first living Earth animal to orbit the planet and experience true weightlessness—although she did not survive the trip. Her spacecraft was *Sputnik 2*, launched one month after *Sputnik 1* and constructed in haste to meet the Soviet Union's political deadlines for national prestige. "Recruited" for training from a compound for stray dogs in Moscow, where she was first called Kudryavka ("Little Curlyhair"), her official name is actually the Russian for a type of dog similar to a husky and means "howler."

———— OLDEST & STRONGEST DOGS ————

DOG RECORDS

Oldest: ADJUTANT, a black labrador belonging to James Hawkes of Lincolnshire, England—37 years 3 months in November 1973 (although the record is often attributed to Bluey, an Australian cattle dog finally put down at 29 years 5 months, an age said to approximate a human age of 129).

Strongest: CHARLIE, an "Arctic dog" (presumably an Alaskan malamute or Siberian husky) who, with many people watching, in Anchor Point, Alaska, in January 1961 apparently pulled a loaded sled weighing 3,560 pounds (1,425 kilos)—1.78 U.S. tons (1.425 metric tonnes).

THE INTERLINGUAL DOG

English . . . *the hound*★
German . . . . *der Hund*
Dutch . . . . . . *de hond*
Danish . . . . . *Hunden*
Norwegian . . . *hunden*
Swedish . . . . . *hunden*
Icelandic . . . . . *hundur*
Esperanto . . . *la hundo*
English . . . *the canine*★
Italian . . . . *Il cane*
Romanian . . . *câine-le*
Albanian . . . . *qeni*
ancient Greek . . *o kuōn*
Portuguese . . . . . *o cão*
Welsh . . . . *ci*
French . . . . . . *le chien*
Sanskrit . . . . *svan*
Latvian . . . . *suns*
Lithuanian . . . . . , *šuo*

★ Note that English *hound*
and *canine* are actually
etymologically cognate

English . . . . *dog*
Dutch . . . . *dog 'mastiff'*
German . . . .
. . . . . . *Dogge 'bulldog'*
Danish . . . .
. . . . . . *Dogge 'mastiff'*

"The dog"
in other languages:

Indonesian/
Malay . . . . *anjing*
Japanese . . . . *inú*
Arabic . . . . *el kalb*
Maltese Arabic . *el kelb*
Hebrew . . . . *ha kelev*
Estonian . . . . *koer*
Finnish . . . . *koira*
Bulgarian . . . *kúche-to*
Hindi . . . . . *yeh kuttaa*
Hungarian . . . *a kutya*
Turkish . . . . *köpek*

Scottish/
Irish Gaelic . . . . *madra*
Thai . . . . *mâh*
Spanish . . . . . . *el perro*
Serbo-Croat . . . . . *pas*
Czech . . . . *pes*
Slovene . . . . *pes*
Polish . . . . *piess*
modern Greek
. . . . : . . . . . . *to skylí*
Russian . . . . . . *sobáka*
Basque . . . . . *txakurra*

WHY THE NAME "DOBERMAN(N)"?

LUDWIG DOBERMANN was a tax collector (and night watchman and municipal dog-catcher) in the township of Apolda, near Weimar in Thuringia, eastern Germany, from the 1840s to the 1890s. Although he was no doubt greatly beloved by all his fellow townspeople, he found that his civic duties required him to be accompanied at all times by a guard dog of elegant yet menacing proportions and, as a part-time dog breeder, he set out to produce one different from any other. It took him 20 years and many genetic combinations, but by the 1880s he had successfully bred what he called the *Dobermannpinscher*, which in English is the Doberman(n) pinscher.

WEIGHTS & BREEDS

Manufacturers of dog foods, dog clothing, dog furniture, and dog accessories tend to work to charts that group dogs by average weight in relation to breed. An example is shown below.

WEIGHT		CLASSIC EXAMPLE BREEDS
1–10 lb **(0.45–5.0 kg)**		*Chihuahuas, Yorkshire terriers, Malteses, Papillons, Pomeranians*
11–25 lb **(5.0–11.5 kg)**		*Dachshunds, Shih Tzus, poodles, pugs, Boston terriers, Bichon frises, miniature pinschers, Lhasa Apsos, French bulldogs, West Highland terriers, Havaneses, Pekingeses, Brussels griffons, Chinese crested dogs*
26–40 lb **(11.5–18.5 kg)**		*Miniature schnauzers, Shetland sheepdogs, beagles, Cavalier King Charles spaniels, Scottish terriers, Cairn terriers, American Staffordshire terriers*
41–70 lb **(18.5–32.0 kg)**		*Bulldogs, boxers, Cocker spaniels, Welsh corgis, basset hounds, Australian shepherd dogs, English springer spaniels, soft-coated wheaten terriers, bull terriers, Shar Peis*
71-90 lb **(32.0–41.0 kg)**		*Golden retrievers, Labradors, Doberman(n) pinschers, Rottweilers, German shepherds, Weimaraners, Siberian huskies, Airedale terriers, wire-haired viszlas, collies, Border collies, Rhodesian ridgebacks, standard poodles, chows*
91–110 lb **(41.0–50.0 kg)**		*Bernese mountain dogs, Alaskan malamutes, Great Danes, Saint Bernards, Old English sheepdogs*

FETCH!

A dog fetches a stick that is thrown by its owner not by watching it and finding it visually but by tracking down the owner's smell that remains on the stick.

THE DOG STAR

SIRIUS, the Dog Star—known technically as *alpha Canis Majoris*—is the brightest star in the night sky, in appearance rivaling even the planets Venus and Jupiter. Its apparent magnitude is -1.46, although this optical brightness is partly due to its comparative closeness to the solar system at a distance of only 8.56 light years (currently the fifth closest stellar entity). It is of spectral type A0, and is a big but not actually gigantic or scorching hot star, with a diameter of around 3 million miles (4.8 million kilometers) and a surface temperature of about 18,032°F (10,000°C). Our own Sun's diameter is about 870,000 miles (1.4 million kilometers) and its surface temperature is about 9,392°F (5,200°C). The Dog Star has a faint companion dwarf star in a complementary orbit (orbital period 50 Earth years), first observed in 1862, now generally known—logically enough—as "the Pup."

MARK TWAIN & THE GATES OF HEAVEN

"Heaven goes by favor. If it went by merit, you would stay out and your dog would go in."

MARK TWAIN (1835–1910) U.S. journalist, writer, and wit

AESOP'S FABLE ABOUT THE OLD DOG

A faithful but elderly dog is gratified to be taken hunting by his aristocratic master. In the course of their excursion through the forest, they come upon a marauding bear, which the dog—knowing that it is expected of him—dutifully attacks. But his teeth are old and fragile, and break, and the bear escapes. The master is considerably annoyed, and punishes the dog. Patiently, and with no small degree of magnanimity, the poor old dog exclaims that at his age he should not be blamed for what he is, but praised for what he used to be.

PUGNAX BRITANNIAE: AN EXTINCT BREED

Among the 21 famous dog breeds that over the centuries have become extinct is the Pugnax Britanniae. Pugnaces Britanniae (*pugnaces* is the plural of *pugnax*, "bellicose") were large fighting dogs with exceptionally wide jaws and were brought from Britain during the first and second centuries CE by the Romans for dogfights in the arena and in war alongside military leaders. Roman writers described them as particularly courageous, persistent, and unusually cunning—more so than any other dogs that existed in Roman times.

PET PARTIES

With an estimated 135,000 dogs, San Francisco has one of the highest per capita populations of dogs of all U.S. cities, according to the San Francisco branch of the Society for the Prevention of Cruelty to Animals. It also has one of the lowest per capita populations of people aged 18 or younger of major U.S. cities, according to the U.S. Census Bureau. This means that pet dogs are treated very, very well. In fact, some might even suggest, tentatively, that they are spoiled rotten.

Bella & Daisy's is a dog boutique on Union Street in San Francisco. The boutique's back room, which normally serves as a full-service day care center for small dogs, is transformed for special clients' birthday parties of up to 10 dogs at a time with streamers, party hats, and snacks. After their human guardians serenade the appropriate one or more canines with the song "Happy Birthday to You," the dogs enjoy cake made from wheat flour, oats, peanut butter, and filtered water. Then the hosts open their "party favors" and gifts—large packages full of chewy toys and other treats.

Parties at the petite storefront boutique cost $200 and include cake, supplies, activities, and the party favors. The shop also offers gift registries on associated items, many of the gifts costing several hundred dollars.

FAVORITE BREEDS: SWEDEN / FINLAND

Most popular breeds since 2006:

IN SWEDEN	IN FINLAND
1. . . . . German shepherd	1. . . . . Finnish hound
2. Labrador	2. . . . . German shepherd
3. . . . . Golden retriever	3. . . . . Labrador
4. . . . . . Swedish elkhound (Jämthund)	4. . . . . Golden retriever
5. . . . . Cocker spaniel	5. . . . . Norwegian elkhound

THE NAMING OF HOUNDSDITCH

HOUNDSDITCH is the name of a wide street in the oldest part of London, England, known as "The City." It follows the path of a defensive ditch around a section of the ancient London Wall first dug in Roman times but extensively renovated when King Canute ruled (1016–35). However, the ditch got its name during the reign of King John (1199–1216), when it was used as a prime site for dumping all kinds of household waste, but particularly dead dogs. The street alongside it was first paved in 1503.

―――――― LEBOWITZ ON EQUITY FOR DOGS ――――――

"If you are a dog and your owner suggests that you
wear a sweater, suggest that he wear a tail."
FRAN LEBOWITZ (b. 1950) *U.S. essayist*

―――――― CHEKHOV'S STORY OF KASHTANKA――――――

Kashtanka was featured in a short story by Russian author Anton Chekhov (1860–1904). She belonged to a drunken and often violent town carpenter. One day she became accidentally separated from her owner and was adopted by the proprietor of a traveling animal show. Life was at once infinitely happier: Kashtanka became part of the show and integrated well with the other animals. Much later, the traveling show returned to that town to perform. The carpenter was in the audience, recognized Kashtanka, and called her name loudly. At once Kashtanka forsook her friends and returned to her wretched life in her original home. The story has various potential morals.

―――――― SOUND BITES ――――――

In the United States, approximately 2 percent of the human population is bitten by dogs each year, but only 17 percent of dog bites are reported.

―――――― THE DOG ROSE ――――――

As a flower, the dog rose—technically *Rosa canina*—has been associated with dogs since it was described as *kuno-rhodon* by the ancient Greeks and as *cynorhodon* in ancient Rome (both intended to mean "dog rose"). In medieval England the flower was featured on heraldic coats of arms, in particular on the badges borne on their outer clothing (and *not* on their shields) by warriors of the Houses of York and Lancaster. Between 1455 and 1487 these warriors disputed the throne of England in the so-called Wars of the Roses (although this term was first popularized only much later in the historical novels of Sir Walter Scott).

It is the dog rose that is the source of rose hips, used in teas and other "rose"-flavored preparations. Rose hips are unusually high in antioxidants and may also be medicinally valuable for their substantial vitamin C content: by weight, rose hips contain up to 50 times the vitamin C found in an orange. However, to obtain that content requires considerable processing, because rose hips are inedible by humans in their raw state—which may well be why they were called dog roses (suitable for dogs to eat raw) in the first place.

DOG DISEASES

Dogs have 200 to 300 diseases in common with humans, including hypotension and cancer — and autoimmune diseases — possibly because they react to their environment in much the same way as humans (which is of course why dogs are occasionally still used in medical research for human treatments). Epilepsy, however, is more common in dogs than it is in humans, and is due to a genetic mutation for which it is now (since January 2005) possible to test dogs before they have had any seizures. Miniature wire-haired dachshunds are particularly susceptible to epilepsy (more than 5 percent of purebreds in the United Kingdom suffer from seizures) of a type that is described as "Lafora disease," a far more serious and, fortunately, far more rare type in humans. Other types of dog susceptible to epilepsy of this kind (which specifically includes seizures brought on by optical conditions such as flashing or pulsing lights) are basset hounds, poodles, and pointers, although all pure breeds are more liable than non-pedigree dogs to seizures because genetic transmission relies on inheritance of the gene from both mother and father.

DOGS ON BOARD THE TITANIC

Two dogs—a Pekingese and a Pomeranian—survived the sinking of the *Titanic* because they were lucky enough to find places with their owners in the very few lifeboats that left the ship early. A third dog, a big Newfoundland, is also rumored to have survived by swimming alongside another lifeboat to which it was instrumental in guiding eventual rescuers.

WHY "POODLE"?

THE POODLE (among the 3 breeds of which the misleadingly named "standard" is in fact the largest) was originally bred as a dog for hunting in rivers and lakes on large estates in Germany and was accordingly called the *Pudelhund*. *Pudel* represents both the English words "puddle" and "paddle," and thus applies simultaneously to the selected environment and the mode of travel through it.

THE LAST BONAPARTE: FELLED BY HIS DOG

Napoleon Bonaparte's last direct descendant (his great-great-nephew) Jérôme Napoleon Bonaparte—born in Massachusetts to a serving U.S. Army officer—died in 1945 at the age of 67 of injuries received when he fell over the outstretched leash of his dog.

STEPHEN FOSTER (1826–1864) wrote many famous tunes—especially what used to be called "negro spirituals," including "The Old Folks at Home," "Camptown Races," "Oh Susannah!," and "Poor Old Joe"—that have been translated and sung in different languages all over the world. He wrote "Beautiful Dreamer," too—but few people know that he also wrote this sentimental song about a dog.

OLD DOG TRAY

The morn of life is past, And eve-ning comes at last; It
The forms I called my own Have van-ished one by one, The
When thoughts re-call the past, His eyes are on me cast— I

brings me a dream of a once hap-py day. Of
loved ones, the dear ones have all passed a- -way; Their
know that he feels what my break-ing heart would say; Al-

man-y forms I've seen Up- - -on the vill- -age gree - - - - - - - -n,
happ-y smiles have flown, Their gen- -tle voi - - ces gone; I've
though he can-not speak, I'll vain- -ly, vain- -ly seek A

Sport-ing with my old dog Tray.
no-thing left but old dog Tray.
bet-ter friend than old dog Tray.

CHORUS: Old dog Tray's ev- -er faith - - - - - - - - - - -ful:

Grief can-not drive him a - - - -way; He's

gen-tle, he is kind— I'll nev- -er, nev- -er find A

bet-ter friend than old dog Tray.

THE DOGO CUBANO: AN EXTINCT BREED

Among the list of 21 famous dog breeds that over the centuries have for one reason or another become extinct is the Dogo Cubano, a type of mastiff bred in Cuba mainly to track and catch runaway slaves. The dogs were simply too expensive to keep after the abolition of slavery, and they quickly died out.

AESOP'S FABLE: THE TRAVELERS

A DOG AND A COCK (that is, a rooster) were friends and traveled together. One evening they found themselves within a thick forest and decided to spend the night in a tree—the dog in the trunk and the cock on a branch above. When the dawn came, the cock crowed—and attracted the attention of a fox, who sauntered up, voiced his admiration, and stated a wish to make his closer personal acquaintance. The cock was suspicious, and he suggested that the fox wake his "porter," sleeping in the trunk below, to let him in. The fox believed the porter would be another bird—but found to his cost that it was the dog, who duly chased him off.

BIBLICAL DOGS

In the Bible, "dog" in the singular is mentioned 15 times, and "dogs" in the plural are mentioned another 15 times. Not every reference is complimentary and, indeed, a few are figurative in meaning, alluding to persecutors, enemies, or low-born riffraff in general. Nor does one quite know what to make of the dog in such declamatorily proverbial statements as: "As a dog returneth to his vomit, so a fool returneth to his folly." (*Proverbs* 26:11) But other than as lions or leopards, cats are not mentioned in the Bible at all.

SAINT BERNARDS & BRANDY KEGS

THE SAINT BERNARD DOG was not named after a saint but after the Great Saint Bernard Pass, in the Swiss Alps, where it was first trained to seek out and rescue travelers caught in winter emergencies. But the pass was named after Saint Bernard of Menthon (or Montjoux or Aosta; died *c.*1081), builder of guesthouses on mountain roads and patron saint of mountaineers.

The popular notion that Saint Bernards carry with them a miniature keg of medicinal brandy derives from the celebrated painting of *St Bernards Reviving a Traveller* by Sir Edwin Landseer (1802–1873), in which one of the dogs does have such a keg. Landseer was better known in his lifetime for painting Newfoundland dogs, one type of which was then named after him.

SHOW CATEGORIES

*The following 7 groups are those most commonly used in shows
organized by national Kennel Clubs around the world:*

1. Sporting dogs
2. Hounds
3. Non-sporting dogs

4. Working dogs
5. Herding dogs

6. Terriers
7. Toy dogs

DOG DAYS

The "dog days" are the hottest, most humid days of summer—the days on which the very idea of doing anything makes you feel dog tired. They were known as "dog days" in the Latin of ancient Rome, but the Romans got the idea from the ancient Greeks (and the ancient Greeks probably got the idea from the ancient Persian Babylonians through their contact with the ancient Egyptians). The idea was astronomical in inspiration, for the dog days were actually the daylight hours of nights on which the Dog Star, Sirius—the brightest star in the Dog constellation—appeared in the form of the Morning Star that blazes low in the sky just before dawn. To the ancient Romans it was a period of exactly 50 days. But to the ancient Greeks, based generally at a lower latitude than Rome, the Dog Star shone just above the horizon for 55 days. And to the Babylonians, based farther south still, it would have been more like 60 days.

Millennia later, in 1552 CE, the *Book of Common Prayer* recorded in its church calendar section that in England the "Dog Daies" were the 40 days between July 6 and August 17, although by then, because of the intervening movement and changes in the heavens since ancient times, the astronomical connection with the Dog Star was of historical and linguistic interest only.

UNMENTIONABLE DOG NAME

It has always seemed strange (if not quaint) to those who are not native French-speakers that *nom d'un chien* is effectively a very mild, and now outdated, expression for swearing— an equivalent perhaps to "Dammit!"

THE GREAT DANE: A CORRECTION

The Great Dane was bred in Germany, not Denmark, and is otherwise known as the "Deutsche Dogge," which translates as German Mastiff.

BARKS AROUND THE GLOBE

Despite considerable differences in spelling, there are only a few variations in how humans around the world write down the sound of a dog barking—and some of them have as much to do with pitch as with pronunciation.

WOOF

Afrikaans	*woef*
Dutch	*woef*
English	*woof, woof-woof*
German	*wuff wuff*
Icelandic	*voff*
Norwegian	*voff, vov-vov*
Swedish, Danish	*vov vov*
Urdu	*woof woof*

BOW, BOW-WOW

Bulgarian	*bau bau*
Catalan	*bup bup*
Croatian	*vau-vau*
English	*bow-wow*
Finnish	*vuh vuh*
German	*wau wau*
Hungarian	*vau-vau*
Hindi	*bho bho*
Italian	*bau bau*
Montenegrin	*vau vau*

WOW/WAU, WAH

French	*ouah ouah*
Vietnamese	*wau wau*

ANOMALOUS ONOMATOPOEIA

English	*arf, ruff ruff, yap, yip*
Indonesian	*guk guk*
Korean	*mung-mung*

HOW/HAU, HOW WOW

Arabic (Algeria)	*haw haw*
Bengali	*ghaue-ghaue*
Czech	*haf haf*
Estonian	*auh*
Finnish	*hau hau*
Greek	*khav*
Hebrew	*haw haw, hav hav*
Montenegrin	*av av*
Polish	*hau hau*
Portuguese (and Brazilian)	*au au au*
Russian	*ghav ghav*
Slovenian	*hov-hov*
Spanish (and Argentinian)	*guau guau*
Turkish	*hav hav*
Ukrainian	*hav-hav*

HAM HAM

Albanian	*ham ham, hum hum*
Romanian	*ham ham*

WAN, WANG

Chinese (Mandarin)	*wang wang*
Japanese	*wanwan, kyankyan*
Korean	*wang-wang*
Thai	*houang houang*

DESPORTES, PAINTER OF DOGS

Not particularly well-known outside France, Alexandre-François Desportes (1661–1743) was the court painter to Kings Louis XIV and XV; he painted their favorite hunting dogs. His animal studies were also featured on valuable Sèvres pottery and Gobelin tapestries.

SENSE OF SMELL

According to one authoritative source, the olfactory receptor cells of the human nose number about 12 million, whereas in most dogs such cells number 1 billion (that is, 83 times more). In a bloodhound, however, there are 4 billion olfactory receptor cells (or 330 times more). Another equally reputable source cites what ought to be the same statistic quite differently: humans have 5 million smell-sensitive cells over a postage-stamp sized area, whereas dogs have 220 million smell-sensitive cells over an area the size of a pocket handkerchief. Either way, dogs can pick up a scent much better than we can—so much better, in fact, that they use the sense of smell in most circumstances in preference to their eyesight, particularly in social contexts, and not just with other dogs. It is through smell, after all, that dogs detect changes of mood in their owners (via the odors contained in sweat and hormonal excretions).

Furthermore, dogs can be trained to use their sense of smell to detect some very unexpected items: not just illegal drugs, explosives, and banknotes, but also cell phones. And recently, dogs have been trained on behalf of medical authorities to act effectively as scanners to detect bladder cancer, some forms of skin cancer, and the incidence of autism in newborn humans.

"A BELL ON THE DOG" EXPLAINED

COCKNEY RHYMING SLANG—a colloquial language still used by some inhabitants of east London, England—demands that the word that actually rhymes is often left unsaid, so that although the slang for "telephone" is "dog and bone," to ask someone to call you, you would say "Give us a bell on the dog." This makes it a guessing game for outsiders to interpret new slang (or indeed, the old slang). If you want to ask, for example, if a person calling you has a cell phone, you would say "You've got a whisky (or an Uncle), haven't you?" Translations: whisky *and soda* (slang for Voda, or Vodafone), Uncle *Toby* (Moby = mobile = cell phone).

GREYFRIARS BOBBY

GREYFRIARS BOBBY was a Skye terrier (originally called "Bobby") who, after his master (a night-watch policeman) John Gray's death in Edinburgh, Scotland, in 1858, refused to leave his graveside in Greyfriars churchyard (or kirkyard) for 14 years other than to eat or find shelter in bad weather, until he himself died and was buried in his own grave in 1872. It was an arrangement supported and partly subsidized by local residents—including the contemporary Lord Provost of Edinburgh—who all regarded the little dog with respect as a notable character of the vicinity. A small commemorative statue to him (1873) stands not far from the comparatively modern gravestone on his grave.

DOG EVOLUTION

At the end of the Mesozoic era, the animals that were to become canids began to spread throughout what is now North America, first in the form of miacids (weasel-like mammals) but gradually evolving (through Hesperocyon, Phlaocyon, Mesocyon, Cynodesmus, Tomarctus, and Leptocyon species) to the true Canidae, which appeared at the end of the Tertiary period. Although initially they were present also in Europe, the rise of larger and ferocious predator competitors such as the bear seems to have wiped out the dogs in Europe for a considerable period of time, until they re-established themselves via the Bering Strait and Asia in the late Miocene epoch. A long time thereafter, canids spread into Africa. But it was not until the early Pleistocene epoch that they reached South America, and it was even later—through human intervention—that they reached Australia.

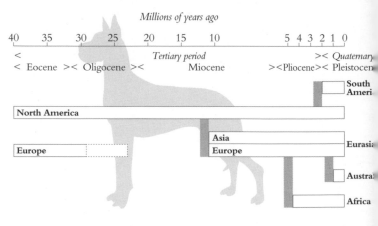

The dingo—often regarded as an Australian native-evolved dog—originated (if that is the correct term for a type of dog that is effectively a reversion to the feral state of a domesticated dog) as the latest "species" of all.

ORIGIN OF THE HOT DOG

As an Americanism for a cooked wiener or frankfurter, especially with onions and mustard (and any other ingredients) between two halves of a bread roll, the hot dog was first immortalized in print in the October 1895 issue of the *Yale Record*, the United States' oldest university campus humor magazine. But the expression originated some 50 years earlier, at a time when sausage-makers were suspected of economizing by using dog meat in their products.

BYRON'S DOG

"Beauty without vanity,
    strength without insolence,
courage without ferocity, and
    all the virtues of man without his vices."
LORD BYRON (1788–1824), *Epitaph for his dog Boatswain*

CANINE DISTEMPER

CANINE DISTEMPER is a disease caused by a single-stranded RNA paramyxovirus, a relative of the measles virus that is harmless to humans. In addition to dogs, however, the virus can cause serious illness in members of the weasel family (especially ferrets), skunks, raccoons, coatis, seals and sea lions, civets, and genets, as well as some of the larger wild cats.

In many jurisdictions of the world, vaccination for dogs against distemper is mandatory. Animals diagnosed as infected must be quarantined for several months because, even after apparently being cured, dogs may remain infectious. However, although mild cases do occur, the majority of infected animals do not survive, partly because the disease encourages secondary bacterial infections that lead to further serious consequences. Moreover, even among urban vaccinated dog populations, outbreaks of distemper may unexpectedly arise (as happened in Finland between 1990 and 1995).

Canine distemper has a long history—which is why it has a name dating from the medieval notion of the 4 humors of the body being kept in temper (or balance)—and seems to have been introduced (or reintroduced) into southern Europe from Peru in the 1750s.

MOSCOW WATER DOG: AN EXTINCT BREED

The Moscow water dog—known alternatively as the Moscow diver or retriever (or the Moskovsky Vodolaz)—was specifically bred to work with the Soviet Union's armed forces as part of a program to replace the military dogs killed during World War II. The intention in this case was to derive a dog that would rescue people from watery environments. The breeding stock was part Newfoundland, part Caucasian shepherd (Ovcharka), and part East European shepherd. Sadly, the program had to be permanently shelved when it was discovered that the dogs successfully produced in Krasnaya Zvezda, Belarus, rather than rescuing the hapless volunteers floundering in the water, tended to attack and bite them instead.

FRENCH PROVERB

The best thing about a man is his dog.

PUPS AT BIRTH

Pups are born unable to see and unable to hear. Initial forms of social interaction manifest for the first time when the puppies are between 14 and 21 days old. Social investigation appears first, followed by attempts at play and by interactions that imply aggression or submission. Barking may begin at as young as 18 days old. By the age of 4 weeks, puppies stand and move like adults. Weaning takes place at 6 weeks.

AESOP'S FABLE: THE DOG AT THE FEAST

A pet dog's master was giving a grand banquet, and the pet dog thereupon invited his canine friend to come too and enjoy the feast. The canine friend did so, but made such a show of strutting around eating his fill as if he were one of the human guests that the cook saw him and was enraged. The dog was thrown out on his ear forthwith. Other dogs of the neighborhood who knew he had been invited to the banquet asked him how he had fared. He said he had eaten and drunk so much that he simply couldn't remember what had happened or how he had managed to get out of the house. Moral: what was more important — to have eaten and drunk or to be able to say you had?

THE CYNICS

In ancient Greece around 400 BCE, a school of philosophy arose around the concept that virtue and self-control were in themselves the greatest rewards in life—the source of all happiness. These ideas were far too idealistic for most people, however, who assumed that adherents of the school were avoiding saying that no one did anything for nothing, and that even apparently altruistic deeds of kindness and charity had to have some underlying selfish motive. The adherents thus quickly became known as the Cynics (*Kunikoi*). However, "the Cynics" description was also a jibe—for *kunikos* is the adjective derived from *kuōn*, "dog," implying that the members of the philosophical school tended to growl "like dogs" at their well-meaning fellow citizens.

It may be testament to the real philosophy of the school that its members accepted and even adopted the name, in due course describing themselves with pride as the Cynics.

POODLE CROSSBREEDS / HYBRIDS

There are more than 60 named crossbreeds involving
a poodle mixed with other breeds:

1. *an Affenpinscher = an Affenpoo*
2. *an Airedale terrier = an Airedoodle*
3. *an American eskimo dog = a Pookimo*
4. *an American rat terrier = a Rattle*
5. *an Australian shepherd = an Aussiedoodle or a miniature Aussiedoodle*
6. *a Basset hound = a Bassetoodle*
7. *a Beagle = a Poogle*
8. *a Bernese mountain dog = a Bernedoodle*
9. *a Bichon and a Shi Tzu = a Daisy dog*
10. *a Bichon frise = a Bich(on)-poo or Poochon*
11. *a Border collie = a Bordoodle*
12. *a Boston terrier = a Bossi-poo*
13. *a Boxer = a Doxenlvodle*
14. *a Brussels griffon = a Broodle griffon*
15. *a Cairn terrier = a Cairnoodle*
16. *a Cavalier King Charles spaniel = a Cavapoo*
17. *a Chihuahua = a Chi-poo*
18. *a Chinese crested = a Chinese crestepoo*
19. *a Cocker spaniel = a Cockapoo*
20. *a Collie = a Cadoodle*
21. *a Coton de tulear = a Poo-ton*
22. *a Dachshund = a Doxiepoo*
23. *a Doberman(n) = a Doodleman*
24. *an English bulldog = an English boodle*
25. *an English springer spaniel = a Springerdoodle*
26. *a Foxhound = a Foxhoodle*
27. *a German shepherd = a Shepadoodle*
28. *a Giant schnauzer = a giant Schnoodle*
29. *a Golden retriever = a Goldendoodle or a miniature Goldendoodle*
30. *a Golden retriever and a Cocker spaniel = a petite Goldendoodle*
31. *a Havanese = a Poovanese*
32. *an Irish setter = an Irish doodle*
33. *an Italian greyhound = a Pootalian*
34. *a Jack Russell = a Jackapoo*
35. *a Japanese Chin = a Poochin*
36. *a Labrador = a Labradoodle or a miniature Labradoodle*
37. *a Labrador and a Cocker spaniel = a petite Labradoodle*
38. *a Lhasa Apso = a Lhasapoo*
39. *a Maltese = a Malti-poo*
40. *an Old English sheepdog = a Sheepadoodle*
41. *a Papillon = a Papi-poo*
42. *a Pekingese = a Pekepoo*
43. *a Pinscher = a Pinny-poo*
44. *a Pomeranian = a Pom(a)poo*
45. *a Pug = a Pugapoo*
46. *a Rottweiler = a Rottle*
47. *a Saint Bernard = a Saint Berdoodle*
48. *a Schipperke = a Schipper-poo*
49. *a Schnauzer = a Schnoodle*
50. *a Scottish terrier (a Scottie dog) = a Scoodle*
51. *a Shar Pei = a Shar-poo*
52. *a Shetland sheepdog = a Sheltidoodle or Sheltipoo*
53. *a Shiba Inu = a Poo-Shi*
54. *a Shih Tzu = a Shih-poo*
55. *a Silky terrier = a Poolky*
56. *a Soft-coated wheaten terrier = a Whoodle*
57. *a Tibetan terrier = a Ttoodle*
58. *a Toy fox terrier (an Amertoy) = a Foodle*
59. *a Weimaraner = a Weimardoodle*
60. *a West Highland terrier = a Westiepoo*
61. *a Yorkshire terrier = a Yorkipoo*

THE ROLE OF DOG SHOW JUDGES

1st prize
TOP DOG

Dog show judges have to be experts on the breeds they are judging. They examine ("go over") each dog with their hands to see if the teeth, muscles, bones, and coat texture conform to the breed's official standard. They view each dog in profile for overall balance, and watch the dog's gait (way of moving) to see how all of those features fit together in action. The judges examine each dog in turn, then allocate awards according to how closely the individual dogs compare to the judge's mental image of the "perfect" dog as described in the official standard. The standard details the characteristics that allow the breed to perform the function for which it was bred, appropriate to the group within which it is competing. Standards include specifications relating to physical form, temperament, and movement. The official written standard for each breed is maintained by the breed's national kennel club, as regularly published and updated.

SINGING DOGS

Dogs appreciate pitch, tone, and volume in what they hear, enabling them to recognize voices, whistles, and even familiar tunes on the radio. But they cannot relate those sound effects to their own vocal apparatus, so they do not actually "sing." Those that appear to try to join in when they hear human singing are in fact setting up a communal howl as they might with the other members of their pack in the wild.

GREYHOUND RACING RULES

In Australian and U.S. greyhound racing the maximum number of runners presently permitted on the track at any one time is 8 dogs, although in former times both 9- and 10-dog races regularly took place. In the United Kingdom, the current maximum number of runners is restricted to 6 dogs, although in the past both 5- and 8-dog greyhound races were once a regular feature.

In greyhound dog racing in England, races are "seeded"—the dogs are allocated to the traps according to how they are known to prefer to race—on the inside, in the middle, or "wide" (on the outside). The racing manager of the course is responsible for organizing and implementing this seeding, and the intention is to avoid collisions and thus enhance safety. In Australian and U.S. racing there is no seeding—any dog can be drawn to run in any post position or from any box number; there is no allocation for preference. A potential consequence (as gamblers should note) is that the trap draw will inevitably favor some racers and disadvantage others, and this will effectively influence the outcome of the race.

POPULAR PETS IN OTHER COUNTRIES

Most popular breeds since 2005:

IN FRANCE	IN SPAIN
1. . . . . *Poodle*	1. *Labrador*
2. . . . . *Labrador*	2. . . . . *German shepherd*
3. . . . . *Yorkshire terrier*	3. . . . . *Yorkshire terrier*
4. . . . . . *Cavalier King Charles spaniel*	4. . . . . *Golder retriever*
5. . . . . *German shepherd*	5. . . . . *Rottweiler*
6. . . . . *Sheepdog (various)*	6. . . . . *Miniature pinscher*
7. . . . . *Toy dog (various)*	7. . . . .*Estrela mountain dog*
8. . . . . *Cocker spaniel*	8. . . . . *Boxer*
9. . . . . *Boxer*	9. . . . .*Portugese podengo*
10. . . . . *Border collie*	10. . . . . *Transmontano mastiff*

BRAIN WEIGHT TO BODY RATIO

The average brain weight to body weight ratio of a dog is 1:125 (whereas the average brain weight to body weight ratio of a human—and of a mouse—is 1:40, and that of a hippo is 1:2,789), but this would seem merely to emphasize either that body size doesn't matter or (as has been accepted since the late nineteenth century) that although brain size is relative in some way to body size, the human brain is exceptionally large, as would appear to be that of a mouse. It should be noted at the same time, however, that brain size does not necessarily correspond to brain complexity or intelligence.

The actual average brain weight of a medium–small dog (e.g., a beagle) is 2½ ounces (72 grams). The average brain weight of a newborn human is 13¼ ounces (375 grams) and of an adult human is 3 pounds (1,350 grams); of an adult elephant it is 10½ pounds (4,780 grams), and of a goldfish it is four hundredths of an ounce (0.1 gram). Each eyeball of an ostrich weighs more than its brain.

NIPPER

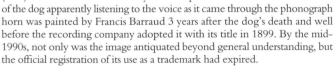

NIPPER was the Jack Russell terrier that was pictured as part of the logo of the *His Master's Voice* (HMV) record label for almost 100 years. The picture of the dog apparently listening to the voice as it came through the phonograph horn was painted by Francis Barraud 3 years after the dog's death and well before the recording company adopted it with its title in 1899. By the mid-1990s, not only was the image antiquated beyond general understanding, but the official registration of its use as a trademark had expired.

WHY "SCHNAUZER"?

"SCHNAUZER" was the actual familiar name of the dog that won Best of Breed when it was first exhibited (as a "wire-haired pinscher") in a show in 1879. It was so called because of its whiskery features emphasized by a prominent nose (*schnauzer* in German is slang for "one with a snout"). Back then—and even after it was introduced to the United States during the 1920s—the breed was classified as a terrier, although now it belongs to the working dogs group.

PAWS & SPOORS

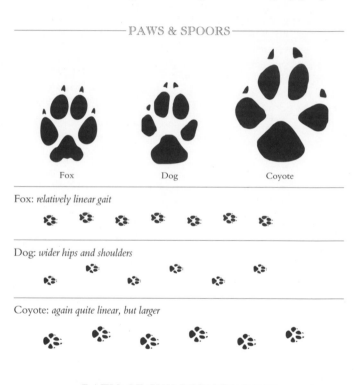

Fox   Dog   Coyote

Fox: *relatively linear gait*

Dog: *wider hips and shoulders*

Coyote: *again quite linear, but larger*

RATIO OF CHILDREN TO DOGS

In 2004, it was announced that there were more dogs in households in the United States and Canada than there were human children.

Alaska is the only state in the U.S. in which there are more dogs per human capita.

CANINE GESTATION

Average gestation time for dogs is 9 weeks but can vary between 58 and 68 days. The mother gains little weight—and doesn't look very different—until after the sixth week of pregnancy. Behavior may at this point change toward restlessness and seeking solitude in a "nest" of shredded paper or torn blankets. Before such signs become evident, however, pregnancy can be confirmed by a vet through careful palpation after 28 to 35 days (with 85 percent accuracy). X-ray diagnosis of the number of puppies is now not advised, but it used to be routinely carried out after about 45 days (with 95 percent mathematical accuracy).

GREETINGS CARDS FROM DOGS

Around 70 percent of dog owners in the United States, when sending birthday or Christmas cards to friends and relatives on behalf of their family, also sign the name of their dog.

AESOP'S FABLE: THE DOG IN THE MANGER

A dog wandered into a barn looking for a place to sleep and found a comfortable bed in a manger full of hay from which the farm cattle were used to eating. He lay down and slept. But when he was woken as the cattle returned to the barn for the night and wanted to eat their hay, he growled and snarled and would not let them near the manger—even though he didn't want to eat the hay himself and had finished using the manger as a bed. It was left to a disconsolate and rather hungry ox to metaphorically shrug his shoulders and say in resignation to his companions, "People all too often resent others getting what they cannot enjoy for themselves."

The fable may or may not be alluded to in the non-canonical *Gospel of Thomas* in a description of the Pharisees by Jesus.

LEONARDO DA VINCI & DOGS

ALTHOUGH LEONARDO DA VINCI (1452–1519) was supremely gifted in being able to draw and paint what he saw, and although he carried out artistic studies of the proportions of a dog's head and of the movements of a dog's paw (or perhaps a wolf), probably the most famous portrait of a dog he is said to have painted—the intendedly jaunty animal accompanying *Tobias and the Angel*—is distinctly less than convincing. But then, that painting is just as often attributed to fellow students of Andrea del Verrocchio (1430s–1480s).

————————— CANINE HEALTH STATISTICS —————————

✳ **Heart rate**: around 180 beats per minute for puppies and toy breeds; 60–160 beats per minute for most adult dogs, although larger dogs tend to have a slower average, of 70–120 beats per minute

✳ **Pulse rate at rest**: 60–120 beats per minute for most dogs (65–80 beats per minute for most adult humans)

✳ **Normal blood temperature**: 100.5–102.5°F (38.0–39.2°C) (for a human: 97.5–99.5°F [36.4–37.5°C])

✳ **Respiration rate**: 16–30 breaths (in and out) per minute when not exercising (for a human: 15–20 breaths per minute when not exercising)

✳ **Œstrus cycle**: 4–6 months

✳ **Œstrus**: 9 days

—— THE TAHLTAN BEAR DOG: AN EXTINCT BREED ——

The Tahltan bear dog was a relatively small, generally black-and-white spitz-type dog descended from primitive pariah migrations across the Bering Strait and used for tracking and hunting bears by the First Nations Indians—most notably the Tahltan Indians—of what is now northwestern Canada (British Columbia and the Yukon). These Ice Age dogs reveled in Arctic conditions but were unable to survive changes in the climate and in the home territory of their human guardians. They were also gradually crossbred out of existence when in more modern times people of other cultures penetrated the area with their domesticated dogs.

————————— THE BADGER HOUND —————————

The word "dachshund" is German for "badger dog," but *Dachs* would only seem to be German, for "badger" was borrowed from another language (most probably an early form of Goidelic Celtic, which has since evolved to become Scottish and Irish Gaelic) in the early centuries CE. In exactly the same way, late Latin borrowed the identical word in the form *taxo* for "badger," having for hundreds of years used the more classical Latin word *meles*. The current German term for the dog is in any case *Dackel* (which looks suspiciously as if it has been partly derived from a Latinate diminutive), hence also French *teckel* and Dutch *tekkel*. Related also to the Latin, though, are words for *dachshund* in Latvian (*taksis*), Lithuanian (*taksas*), Estonian (*taksi-koer*, where *koer* is "dog"), Russian (*taksa*), and Swedish (*tax*).

Interestingly, the original Goidelic Celtic word may or may not have meant "earth-mover" (compare to English *dig, ditch,* and *dyke*) and in addition to the badger may have applied equally to the mole.

―――――― DOG BITES: MAN'S BEST FRIEND? ――――――

Around 90 percent of all dog bites happen to people who know the dog.

―――――― RECOMMENDED KENNEL SIZES ――――――

It is essential that a kennel for a dog is of the correct size—and that the correct size accords not only with the spatial dimensions of the dog but also with its weight. A small, light dog needs (and is happier to reside in) less space than a small but comparatively heavy dog. The floor areas below, derived from kennel manufacturers' statistics, are therefore simply generalized averages, although the manufacturers of course meant them as recommendations. No height for a kennel is given.

Size of dog	Weight of dog	Recommended area of kennel
small and light	1–10 lb (0.45–5.0 kg)	19 x 13 in (48 x 33 cm)
small/heavy to medium/light	11–25 lb (5.0–11.5 kg)	24 x 18 in (61 x 46 cm)
medium/light to medium/heavy	26–40 lb (11.5–18.5 kg)	30 x 20 in (76 x 51 cm)
medium/heavy to large/light	41–70 lb (18.5–32.0 kg)	36 x 23 in (91 x 59 cm)
large/light to large/heavy	71–90 lb (32.0–41.0 kg)	42 x 28 in (106 x 71 cm)
large/heavy to monster	91–110 lb (41.0–50.0 kg)	48 x 30 in (122 x 76 cm)

―――――― SAMUEL BUTLER ON THE DOG ――――――

"The great pleasure of a dog is that you may make a fool of yourself with him and not only will he not scold you, but he will make a fool of himself too."
SAMUEL BUTLER (1835–1902) *English author*

HERRICK'S LAMENT

"Now that you are dead, no eye will ever see Spaniel
with your shape and your service. My love offers a tear
to your sad death, even when it deserves a million."

ROBERT HERRICK (1591–1674)
English poet and priest (Epitaph: *Upon my Spaniel, Tracie*; 1648)

SKIJORING

Skijoring is a winter sport that involves a person on skis being towed along a snow-covered track at the end of a rope by one, two, or 3 dogs in a harness. With one or two dogs, the skier usually skis in either the "classic" or the more modern "skate-skiing" technique, and is given extra speed and mobility by the dogs; with 3 dogs greater speed may actually be achieved if the skier remains rigid and is simply towed along. The rope is attached to the skier by a quick-release clip on a wide belt-sash or waistband. As a sport, skijoring has a comparatively long history; it first came to international attention when it was a demonstration sport at the first Winter Olympic Games held in St. Moritz, Switzerland, in 1928. The sport's name is an adapted version of the Norwegian *skikjøring*, "ski-driving."

GREYHOUND COLORATION

*The American Greyhound Track Operators Association
officially recognizes 18 different colorations of greyhounds★:*

1. . . . . black	7. . . . . . dark brindle	13. . . . . . . red and white
2. . . . black & white	8. . . . . dark red	14. . . . . red brindle
3. . . . . black brindle	9. . . . . fawn	15. . . . . red fawn
4. . . . . .blue	10. . . . .fawn brindle	16. . . . . . . white & black
5. . . . . . blue brindle	11. . . . . light brindle	17. . . . . .white & brindle
6. . . . . .brindle	12. . . . . .red	18. white & brindle-ticked

★ The Association leaves an additional class open for "other colors."

THE SHEEPDOG'S STARE

A GOOD SHEEPDOG has to have "eye." This is a transfixing stare that the dog can bring to bear on sheep in order to compel them to move in the desired direction. However, a dog with too much "eye" can itself become transfixed—standing rooted to the spot, staring at the sheep with a fixed gaze and ignoring any further commands.

─────── PICKLES: FINDER OF THE WORLD CUP───────

PICKLES was the mongrel dog who discovered the Jules Rimet Trophy (the World Cup soccer trophy) that had been stolen a week before from an exhibition in Central Hall, Westminster, London, in March 1966. To the disgust of the contemporary cup-holders, Brazil—who had forwarded the trophy for the exhibition, and who said that the theft could never have happened in Brazil—the solid gold cup was stolen from under the noses of at least two security guards. A ransom attempt was made and a suspect was arrested. Possibly following a plea bargain between the suspect and the police legal department, and through the activity of a third party trusted by both, the trophy was said to be "recoverable." And soon afterward Pickles—out for a walk with his master in Norwood, south London—sniffed out the cup, which was wrapped in newspaper under a hedge. Some months later it was presented to the victorious England team at Wembley Stadium. Seventeen years later, the same trophy was again stolen—in Brazil—and has since never been recovered. Evidently, there was no Brazilian equivalent of Pickles.

─────── ── WHY "ROTTWEILER"? ───────

The Rottweiler is named after the town of Rottweil ("red village") in southwestern Germany, on the bank of the River Neckar, in the state of Baden-Württemberg, population (2006) 25,600. Despite the town's relatively modern German name, it came to prominence as long ago as 73 CE, when the Romans enlarged it as a waystation for cattle-drovers on the road to Württemberg—and the dog seems to have been used in the region since Roman times primarily to assist with the cattle herding. This is why it used more formally to be called the Rottweiler *Metzgerhund* ("butchers' dog").

─────── COCKER / WESTIE CROSSBREEDS / HYBRIDS ───────

Each has 7 named crossbreeds:

A COCKER SPANIEL &
1. an American eskimo dog
   = a Cockamo
2. a Beagle = a Bocker
3. a Bichon frise = a Cockachon
4. a Golden retriever = a Cogol
5. a Pekingese = a Cockinese
6. a Pomeranian = a Cockeranian
7. a Yorkshire terrier = a Corkie

A WEST HIGHLAND TERRIER &
1. a Bichon frise = a Weechon
2. a Cairn terrier = a Cairland terrier
3. a Maltese = a Highland maltie
4. a Miniature schnauzer = a Wauzer
5. a Pug = a Pugland
6. a Shih Tzu = a Weshi
7. a Yorkshire terrier
   = a Westshire terrier

DOG EAR, SOUTH DAKOTA

D og ear is a rural township in Tripp County, South Dakota, made up of 14 houses and 6 mobile homes. Population recorded at the turn of the millennium: 62 (34 females of average age 33; 28 males of average age 37). Elevation: 2,375 feet (724 meters). Average household annual income is about half the national average, although nobody is registered as living below the official poverty line. At least 70 percent of the residents claim to be of German ancestry, 14 percent to be of Irish; some other residents are of Native American or Alaskan Indian extraction.

DOGS & HUMAN ALLERGIES

People who suffer from allergic reactions when in contact with dogs are almost always hypersensitive to what is on the dog's hair—dust, pollen, and the equiv-alent of dandruff—and not to the hair itself. Consequently, larger dogs and dogs that are particularly hairy are those likely to cause the most problems because they shed proportionately more of those allergenic particles into the air and onto surrounding surfaces.

The top 10 dogs recommended as "hypoallergenic" are:

1 . . . . *Bedlington terrier*	6 . . . . *Maltese*
2 . . . . *Bichon frise*	7 . . . . *Poodle*
3 . . . . *Chinese crested dog*	8 . . . . *Portuguese water dog*
4 . . . . *Irish water spaniel*	9 . . . . *Schnauzer*
5 . . . . *Kerry blue terrier*	10 . . . . *Soft-coated wheaten terrier*

Conversely, dogs to avoid as potentially "hyperallergenic" include German shepherds, basset hounds, Cocker spaniels, Afghan hounds, dachshunds, and Irish setters.

PLATO, ON CANINE CONTEMPLATION

"A dog has the soul of a philosopher."
PLATO (*c.* 427–347 BCE) *Greek philosopher*

DOG BITES & BELGIANS

In Belgium in the year 2000, 1 in 100 humans in rural areas had been bitten by a dog in the previous year—in cities the figure was strangely much lower: 1 in 200, mostly in the age group 35 to 44.

THE UNCOMMUNICATIVE DOG

Other than for basic canine sounds of fear, fright, pain, sorrow and anger, dogs do not usually resort to vocal expression. They are thought to have a maximum of only 10 distinct vocal sounds available to them (whereas cats, for example, have more than 100).

AESOP'S FABLE: THE DOG & THE OYSTER

A dog swallows an oyster under the impression it is his favorite food, an egg. When he gets a painful stomachache soon after, he acknowledges his lack of discrimination: those who act without attention to the present or foresight for the future do but bring trouble upon themselves.

DOMESTIC DISEASE SPREAD TO WILDLIFE

In some areas of the world, the domestic dog has been responsible for introducing canine distemper to wildlife previously unexposed to the viral disease. In 1991, for example, the lion population in the Serengeti National Park, Tanzania, underwent a 20 percent decline as a result of an outbreak of the disease primarily among local dogs but (and probably consequently) also among the bat-eared foxes and spotted hyenas in the park.

THE BRISTOL BULLDOG

THE BRISTOL BULLDOG, a single-seater fighter biplane, was the most widely used aircraft by the British Royal Air Force (RAF) between World Wars I and II. Designed by the Bristol Aeroplane Company, the prototype first flew in May 1927. Its 450-horsepower Jupiter engine gave it a maximum speed of just under 180 mph (290 km/h) and a range of 300 miles (480 kilometers). Its armory comprised two Vickers .303-inch (7-millimeter) machine guns and it had capacity for carrying up to four 20-pound (9-kilogram) bombs. Its aircraft maintenance was relatively easy and cheap, which made it popular with air forces around the world, especially those in Scandinavian countries, Spain, and Japan. Mass production began in 1928, but such was the speed of advancement in technology and materials that it was as early as 1937 that the Bulldog was finally withdrawn from RAF service, having been overtaken in several respects by the Hawker Hurricane and the Supermarine Spitfire, which were to undertake even more demanding service during World War II, which began only a short time afterward.

A SHEEPDOG TRIALS COURSE

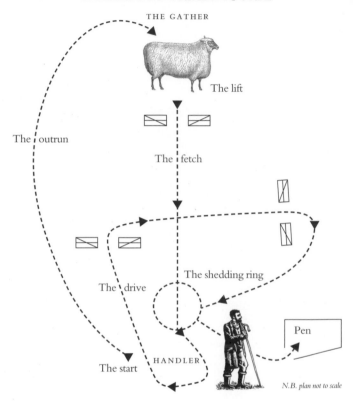

THE GATHER

The lift

The outrun

The fetch

The shedding ring

The drive

The start

HANDLER

Pen

N.B. plan not to scale

In most areas of the world where sheepdogs are used on a daily basis (including Canada and Jamaica), the sheepdog trials course is in keeping with those found in sheepfarming regions of the United Kingdom. The outrun is thus of about 440 yards (400 meters), the fetch about 350 yards (315 meters) and the drive about 150 yards (140 meters). One sheep has to be temporarily but distinctly separated from the others in the shedding ring

before all are driven into the pen. Points are deducted from a maximum total for each maneuver as faults are detected by the judges. In Australia, however, a trial (singular) course is slightly simpler, containing a race (a constricted passage) and a bridge but no shedding ring, and the handler — there called "the worker"—has to walk considerably farther for part of the time, followed by the sheepdog keeping close control of the sheep.

CRUFTS DOG SHOW

C RUFTS DOG SHOW, held annually in London, England, is officially recognized by the *Guinness Book of World Records* as the world's largest pedigree dog show. In 2008 some 25,000 dogs were entered, including around 1,000 dogs from overseas. Over the 4 days, the 7 different pedigree dog groups are shown, and every day, as each group is judged, a Best in Group winner is chosen. These winners go on to compete in the grand finale on the last evening of the show for the ultimate title of Best in Show. Simultaneously, other competitions take place, including the international obedience, agility, and heelwork to music competitions. Crufts, founded in 1886 by entrepreneur Charles Cruft, is now controlled by the (U.K.) Kennel Club—whose annual show for crossbreeds and mongrels is accordingly called Scruffts.

RECIPE FOR A DOG BISCUIT

A basic recipe calls for:
* ✳ *3½ cups chicken stock or beef stock, the richer the better*
* ✳ *1 package of dry yeast*
* ✳ *3½ cups unbleached flour*
* ✳ *1¾ cups whole-wheat flour*
* ✳ *generous 1 cup cornmeal (ground maize, not cornflour)*
* ✳ *⅔ cup skim milk powder*
* ✳ *egg wash (raw egg beaten with a little water and salt)*

Warm the broth until lukewarm, and dissolve the yeast in it. Let the mixture sit for 10 minutes or so while you stir all of the other dry ingredients together in a separate bowl. Then add the yeasty stock to the flour-meal-milk mix, stirring it in to make a dough that can be rolled out flat to a thickness of a quarter of an inch (6 millimeters). Cut biscuit shapes from the dough (there should be enough for around 60 of medium size) and brush each lightly on both sides with egg wash. Bake on greased cake pans or on greased foil at 300°F (150°C) for 45 minutes. Turn the oven off at that point but leave the biscuits inside overnight to harden.

CANINE DENTITION

PUPPIES have 28 teeth (12 incisors, 4 canines, and 12 premolars) and adult dogs have 42 (12 incisors, 4 canines, 16 premolars, and 10 molars). Puppies usually lose their deciduous (milk or baby) teeth at around 6 months—incisors first, canines last—although it is not uncommon for one or more deciduous teeth to be retained if the succeeding adult tooth is misaligned. A retained tooth that causes dental problems must be extracted.

DOGVILLE, THE MOVIE

Dogville (2003, directed by Lars von Trier, founder of the Dogme 95 stylized filmmaking movement) starred Nicole Kidman as a mysterious woman who in the Depression era seeks sanctuary from her Mob connections in a small Rocky Mountain community (Dogville, "a quiet little town not far from here"), only to find that the people's welcome has strings attached that are progressively and eventually inhumanely unpleasant. Lauren Bacall and James Caan also starred.

FAVORITE BREEDS: DENMARK / ICELAND

Most popular dog breeds since 2007:

IN DENMARK	IN NORWAY
1. . . . . *German shepherd*	1. . . . . *German shepherd*
2. . . . . *Norwegian elkhound*	2. . . . . *Golden retriever*
3. . . . . *English setter*	3. . . . . *Norwegian elkhound*

WHY "DANDIE DINMONT" TERRIER?

DANDIE DINMONT was a character in Sir Walter Scott's novel *Guy Mannering* (1814)—a rural farmer who owned 6 of the distinctive terriers. Scott described them so well and with such sentimental feeling that not only did the breed instantly thereafter become known by the name of the farmer but the two names the farmer ascribed to the 6 dogs (Pepper and Mustard) became the official description of the two coloration schemes of the terriers.

"Dandie" is a Scottish pet form of the name Andy, short for Andrew. The Dandie Dinmont remains the only breed named after a fictional character.

THE WOLF-MOTHER

According to ancient tradition, Romulus and Remus (the baby sons of Rhea Silvia and the god Mars), having been set adrift in the River Tiber in a basket that then came ashore, were found and suckled by a she-wolf, and so avoided the death intended for them. The bronze statue of the wolf suckling the boys remains one of the most famous today in Rome, Italy, the city that Romulus was eventually to found. However, the story may be no more than a misinterpretation of an alternative tradition—that the boys were reared instead by one Acca Larentia, who was either a form of the goddess Lupa ("she-wolf") or was actually no more than a courtesan (Latin slang *lupa*, literally "she-wolf").

INFLATIONARY FEARS

"My dog is worried about the economy because Alpo is
up to 99 cents a can. That's almost $7 in dog money."
JOE WEINSTEIN (b. 1953) *U.S. humorous writer*

THE CHOW'S BLACK TONGUE

The chow is often described as the only dog
(sometimes the only animal) to have a black
tongue rather than a pink one, but this is a fallacy.
The Chinese Shar Pei is another dog that has a
black tongue (and giraffes, polar bears, and some
cattle also have black tongues). The reason for the
black tongue remains unknown—but it should
be noted in the meantime that chow puppies' tongues are pink at birth and
gradually darken to blue-black by around 10 weeks. Even then, the tongues
may not turn completely black but retain pinkish spots or streaks.

CANINE GIANT

Believed to be the largest dog on record, Duke—a Saint Bernard belonging
to Dr. A. M. Bruner of Oconomowuc, Wisconsin—weighed in at
390 pounds (135 kilograms) in 1965.

ALBRECHT DÜRER & DOGS

One of the 60 known works by the master draughtsman Albrecht Dürer
(1471–1528) is the brush and ink study of *A Greyhound* (1500). The
outline was indented with a stylus because it was intended to impress it onto
a sheet below and to use that for engraving the design within a much larger
picture called *The Vision of St. Eustace* that he finished a year later. A dog also
appears in each of the 3 "master engravings" on copper that he completed in
1513–14: the *Knight, Death, and Devil* (possibly Dürer's most famous work
other than *Praying Hands*), *St. Jerome in His Study*, and *Melencolia I*. Some
commentators have suggested that it is the same dog in each of the 3 works
but portrayed at different ages.

A CYNICAL PORTUGUESE PROVERB

"The dog wags his tail not for you but for your bread."

THE CANINE SIXTH SENSE

Dogs are renowned for having a "sixth sense" by which they are, for example, aware of the precise time the master starts home from work in the evening. It is not enough to say that dogs use signals from the environment (magnetic changes, minute earth tremors, anticipation on the part of nearby humans or other animals) to be aware of impending events. Dogs can and do take notice in such ways but there would seem to be responses to imminent events and incidents for which there can be no such warning signals and that they are nonetheless aware of. However, the enhanced 4 out of 5 senses of a dog (all but taste) may be enough to explain many such responses that seem to suggest a sixth sense. Moreover, it is part of the human liking for dogs that we want them to be special. After all, it is possible for humans to train themselves to be far more attuned to nature, and thus know when natural events are likely to occur, without having to marvel at a dog's super-sensitivity.

THE HAWAIIAN POI: AN EXTINCT BREED

THE HAWAIIAN POI DOG was a pariah dog (a dog not kept in households but living in association with humans, partly as scavengers) that earned its keep in Hawaiian island communities sometimes by nannying children and sometimes by being fattened up and eaten. In this latter capacity, the diet fed to the dogs consisted mainly of pureed taro root, locally known as *poi*—hence the name of the dog. The dogs were consequently mostly stocky, short-legged, fat, slow, and of lazy temperament and dull intellect. This contributed to their extinction as a distinct breed halfway through the nineteenth century, as did interbreeding with dogs brought in by folk from other parts of the world. "Poi dog" remains a term for "mongrel" in Hawaii.

SHEEPDOG COMMANDS

The classic commands as used by shepherds and handlers in most of the world (and which at distance are replaced by special coded whistles) are:

"Away," "Away to me" . . . . circle the sheep from right to left
"Come by" . . . . circle the sheep from left to right
"Stand". . . . . stop dead
"Get back," "Get out". . . . . .allow the sheep more space
"In," "In here" .intervene between sheep at once
"Lie down" . . . . stop, stay still, or go very slowly
"Walk up," "Walk on". . . . . approach the sheep slowly but directly

—— AESOP'S FABLE: THE BLIND MAN & THE CUB——

A blind man is brought a wolf cub and asked to say what it is. He feels it and says it is either a young wolf or a fox or a dog—but in every case it is an animal not to be let free in a sheep-pen. The moral is that even when not recognized immediately, evil tendencies cannot be hidden for long.

————————— THE SPORT OF DISC DOG —————————

Disc dog is actually better known around the world as "frisbee dog," but that term is frowned on by those who run competitions because it mentions a registered trademark name that is the property of the Wham-O company. Yet a human throwing a Frisbee (all right, a "flying disc") for a dog to catch is what it's all about. There are 3 types of contest. Toss and Fetch (alternatively called Throw and Catch or Minidistance) awards points for successful catches at various specified distances. Long Distance events have many formats, but in general the farthest distance at which the Frisbee is caught wins. Finally, there is the Dynamic Freestyle, which involves a rehearsed routine of up to 3 minutes' duration set to music and utilizing a number of Frisbees all at the same time: points are awarded on a relatively subjective basis by judges but according to several technical points scales including marks for (canine) agility and degree of difficulty.

————————————— RABIES —————————————

Rabies, or hydrophobia, is a viral disease that (unless treated very quickly after infection) causes encephalitis and death in unvaccinated humans. The virus involved would seem to be a mutated form of a bat-vectored RNA virus evolutionarily aimed at infecting plants but that now infects mammals, notably dogs (but also cats, foxes, skunks, raccoons, cattle, and monkeys), which in turn pass the virus on via the saliva through a bite on a human. In the absence of an obvious bite, diagnosis in humans is complicated on account of the huge number of other potential causes of viral encephalitis. Yet because the transmission of the virus is possible in saliva and other body fluids, human-to-human infection by intimate personal contact is technically feasible if either party has not been vaccinated.

The symptoms of rabid encephalitis are generally present between 2 and 12 weeks after infection, but once symptoms have appeared, death is likely within 10 days. Flu-like symptoms turn into partial paralysis, mental dysfunction, and the over-secretion of saliva that, with paralysis of the throat, cannot be swallowed (causing "foaming at the mouth"), leading to a sensation of drowning (thus hydrophobia, or "fear of water").

BYRON'S COMMENDATION

"The poor dog, in life the firmest friend,
The first to welcome, foremost to defend . . ."
LORD BYRON (1788–1824) *English poet*

GREYHOUND RACING COLORS

EVERY GREYHOUND RACING NATION has its own system of colors for racing jackets, blankets, and rugs that denote the "post" (the trap or box) from which each individual greyhound is to begin a race. After all, it is extremely important for trackside gamblers to be able to identify racing dogs (and weigh up their chances) beforehand and for spectators to be able to follow any selected dog once the race is ongoing. Two good examples are the systems of the United Kingdom (adopted by much of Europe) and the United States.

TRAP NO.	USA	UK
1	red	red
2	blue	blue
3	white	white
4	green	black
5	black	orange
6	yellow	black/white stripes
7	green/white stripes	—
8	black/yellow hoops	—

The system used in Australia is different again, officially involving the colors for 9 traps. Perhaps the best-known of its variants is the pink jacket for trap no. 8.

DOG-OWNING HOUSEHOLDS

At the turn of the millennium, 13.3 percent of households in Germany contained at least 1 dog, as did 27.8 percent of households in France and 18.3 percent of households in Japan. In the Netherlands there were 9.4 dogs (and 14.4 cats) for every 100 human residents, and in Belgium there were 10.4 dogs (and 16.3 cats) for every 100 human residents. In the United States the average number of dogs in a dog-owning household was 1.41.

SNOOPY: A COMPLEX CHARACTER

Snoopy was the pet beagle drawn as the major proponent other than the human anti-hero Charlie Brown in an intimate and funny cartoon series (*Peanuts*) by Charles M. Schultz from 1950 to the 1990s. The series was initially based on memories of Schultz's own childhood pets Snooky and Spike. Famous for such sentimental epithets as "Happiness is a warm puppy," Schultz (1922–2000) nonetheless gave Snoopy a comparatively complex and literate character, saying of the dog: "He has to retreat into his fanciful world in order to survive. Otherwise, he leads a kind of dull, miserable life."

WHY "SPANIEL"?

The Norman French conquerors of England in 1066 brought with them a type of dog they had recently also introduced to France, and that they believed originated in Spain. They therefore described the dog (in medieval French) as *espaigneul*, "Spanish"—the pronunciation of which was almost identical with the current English pronunciation of "spaniel." Variants of the English word are now used in most European languages (even in Spanish) for the dog, although in modern French the word has elided to *épagneul*.

BICHON / YORKIE CROSSBREEDS / HYBRIDS

Each has 13 named crossbreeds/hybrids:

a Bichon frise &
a Beagle = a Glechon
a Cairn terrier = a Kashon
a Chihuahua = a Chichon
a Cocker spaniel = a Cockachon
a Havanese = a Havachon
a Japanese Chin = a Ja-Chon
a Lhasa Apso = a La-Chon
a Maltese = a Maltichon
a Pekingese = a Peke-a-chon
a Pomeranian = a Bichon-aranian
a Shih Tzu = a Zuchon
a Toy fox terrier = a Fochon
a West Highland terrier
   = a Weechon

a Yorkshire terrier &
a Bichon frise = a Yochon
a Cairn terrier = a Carkie
a Chihuahua = a Chorkie
a Cocker spaniel = a Corkie
a Japanese Chin = a Jarkie
a Lhasa Apso = a Yorkie-Apso
a Maltese = a Malkie
a Miniature schnauzer = a Snorkie
a Pekingese = a Yorkinese
a Pomeranian = a Yoranian
a Pug = a Pugshire
a Shih Tzu = a Shorkie Tzu
a West Highland terrier
   = a Westshire terrier

THE CYNOSURE

In English, a "cynosure" is a focal point, a center of attraction, a fascinating sign or direction. But if you look up the English word in a good foreign-language dictionary, you will find it given the additional meanings either of the constellation Ursa Minor (the Lesser Bear) or of its best-known star, Polaris, the Pole Star. It is in connection with Polaris—a star that gives a good indication to travelers, especially sailors, of the direction of north— that cynosure has its ordinary meaning in English. It was Polaris (with or without its nearest stars) that was known to the ancient Greeks as *Kunosoura*, and to the Romans in Latin soon afterward as *Cynosura*. And that is strange, because *Kunosoura* means "Dog's tail," and neither Polaris nor Ursa Minor is recorded as ever having been part of a super-constellation known as The Dog. None of the 3 northern "dog" constellations known to the Romans and retained by astronomers today is anywhere near.

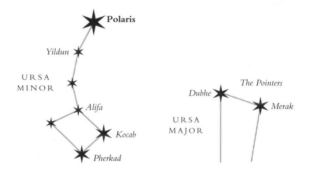

DOGTOWN, U.S.

There have been 6 communities so called in the United States. Three remain solely as ghost towns (two in California, one in Massachusetts). One is an area/suburb of Oakland, California, and another is an "unincorporated community" in West Marin (rural Marin County, California). The last has been renamed Magalia, in California. In former times another small community of this name existed temporarily during the Gold Rush era in the north of San Joaquin County, California. Meanwhile, the area surrounding Drake University in Des Moines, Iowa, is also sometimes today called Dogtown because the school's mascot is the bulldog. Moreover, "Dogtown" as a nickname is sometimes similarly applied to the Clayton/Tamm neighborhood of St. Louis, and to north Little Rock, Arkansas.

DO DOGS CLIMB TREES?

Individuals may learn to, and do it for fun—but in general, dogs do not climb trees. This is because in nature the animals they hunt (mainly deer and small mammals, when they are not simply scavenging) do not climb trees either. Moreover, most dogs are confident that, when necessary, they can run away fast enough rather than have to escape upward. One consequence is that dogs bury food—notably bones—rather than keeping aerial larders in trees, as some wildcats do.

AESOP'S FABLE: THE DOG'S REFLECTION

A dog carrying a large chunk of meat he has scavenged hurries homeward across a rickety bridge over a stream. Halfway across, he looks down into the water—and sees a dog just like himself, with a large chunk of meat. At once he drops his own burden and jumps into the water to get the other dog's meat also. He very quickly discovers that there is no other dog, no other meat, and he has lost his own meat now too. He trudges on sadly home, where he indulges in a different sort of reflection—that "it is pointless to lose the substance by grasping at the shadow."

DOG SHOW ROSETTES & RIBBONS

DOG SHOWS, run under the auspices of national kennel clubs, all tend to use the same system of colored rosettes and ribbons as awards, although the larger shows (such as Crufts in England and Westminster in the United States) generally present silver cups, crystal glassware, or other forms of trophy in addition.

- ❀ **blue rosette:** *winner of individual class; winner of group competition*
- ❀ **red rosette:** *runner-up in individual class; runner-up in group competition*
- ❀ **yellow rosette:** *third in individual class; third in group competition*
- ❀ **white rosette:** *fourth in individual class; fourth in group competition*
- ❀ **purple ribbon:** *winners of Winners Dog/Winners Bitch classes*
- ❀ **purple & white ribbon:** *Reserve Winners—runners-up in Winners Dog/ Winners Bitch classes*
- ❀ **blue & white ribbon:** *Best of Winners—the better of the Winners Dog/ Winners Bitch winners*
- ❀ **purple & gold ribbon:** *Best of Breed winner (in each breed competition)*
- ❀ **red & white ribbon:** *Best of Opposite Sex—awarded to a dog of the same breed as the Best of Breed winner but of the opposite sex*
- ❀ **red, white & blue ribbon:** *winner of Best in Show*

FAVORITE BREEDS: ITALY / IRELAND

Most popular breeds in 2006—in no particular order:

IN ITALY
* Border collie
* Rottweiler
* Boxer
* Great Dane
* Cane Corso (Italian mastiff)
* American Staffordshire terrier
* Jack Russell terrier
* Dachshund

IN IRELAND
* Cavalier King Charles spaniel
* West Highland terrier
* Labrador
* Boxer
* Shih Tzu
* Soft-coated wheaten terrier
* German shepherd
* Irish setter

MICROCHIP RECOGNITION

Most purebred dogs now have a radio-frequency identification (RFID) microchip implanted in the loose skin at the shoulder so that their home details are readily available should any question arise. The chip, with a capacitor and tiny aerial, is encased in a hermetically sealed tube made of biologically inert soda lime glass, no larger than a grain of uncooked rice. When a scanner emitting radio waves of very low frequency is passed over the chip, the aerial detects the waves and the chip's transponder reveals its identification number on the scanner's readout. That unique number is listed against the owner's name and address in the regional/national dog microchip database.

WHOSE BEST FRIEND?

"Properly trained, a man can be a dog's best friend."
COREY FORD (1902–1969) *U.S. short-story and screenplay writer*

CANICROSS: A SPORT FOR MAN & HIS DOG

Canicross is a winter sport in which a human cross-country runner is "assisted" by being consistently pulled forward by one or more dogs on a harness at the end of a rope line attached by a quick-release clip to the runner's waistband—although with only one dog, a simple leash might be sufficient. The effort made by the dog or dogs is intended both to reduce the effort made by the human runner and to extend the length of the runner's strides, so increasing speed and overall distance covered.

FASTEST SPEED

A greyhound's top speed is about 22 yards (20 meters) per second (45 mph [72 km/h]) over 440 yards (400 meters), although Salukis and Afghan hounds are almost as fast and able to maintain that sort of speed for slightly longer.

THE SHISA OF OKINAWA

The *shisa* are iconic lion-dogs that sit in pairs on household rooftops or on both sides of household gates all over the Okinawan islands of Japan. The female shisa's mouth is open, inviting the approach of good luck and warning off evil influences; she sits on the right. The male shisa's mouth shows clenched teeth in a snarl or perhaps a taut grin, said to be holding the good luck in; he sits on the left. Together, they represent an element of spiritual protection for the household, and yet their appearance is light-hearted, if not actually comical—a contrast that is held to reflect the general disposition of the Okinawan islanders. Nonetheless, the tradition of the shisa was in fact borrowed in ancient times from the culture of mainland China and its *fu* dogs, which are still regarded today as household "enhancers" by practitioners of and advisers on *feng shui* worldwide.

DOG BITES & CHILDREN

In the United States every year, nearly 800,000 dog bites on humans are serious enough to require medical attention. About half of these dog bites are made on children, and some 4 out of 10 of those cause the loss of some facial tissue and may result in scarring.

MECHANICAL USES OF THE DRIVE DOG

A drive dog is an attachment on an electrical or mechanical machine in which the major motive force is rotational (as on a lathe or a drill); it transfers or assists the application of the powered rotation to the item that has to be turned, thus minimizing torque.

On a lathe, a drive dog is locked into one turning end via a rod extension that fits into a faceplate, but is also screw-fixed onto the item to be turned so that the turning motion is consistently applied (with no twist or torque). The drive dog and faceplate are otherwise freestanding parts used only as necessary.

On the kind of robust sewing machine used by upholsterers, a drive dog is a standard part that attaches to and assists the turning of the bobbin.

PAVLOV & HIS DOGS

IVAN PETROVICH PAVLOV (1849–1936) was a Russian physiologist and physician whose major work turned out to be fundamental to some aspects of psychology. It was for his research into digestive processes that he received the Nobel Prize in 1904. But it was that same research that prompted him to ask how it was that in dogs the anticipation of food could initiate the production of gastric secretions. So began his study of what he called "conditional reflexes" in dogs, and what others mistranslated, a decade or more later, as "conditioned reflexes." The resultant notion of "conditioning" became a key concept in the form of psychology known as behaviorism.

It should be noted, however, that if Pavlov had tried to carry out his experiments on dogs anywhere in the Western world after the 1970s, he would probably have been prosecuted for animal cruelty (since he was specifically testing the animals themselves and not testing any potentially remedial substance or methodology on behalf of human therapies). Virtually all of the dogs that contributed to his studies in psychological conditioning died as a result, many of them suffering miserably first.

THE COST OF OWNING A DOG

In 2007, it was calculated in the United States that the average overall cost of owning a dog (which lives for an average 11 years) was $13,350—or $3.30 a day, for every day of its life.

WHY "SPITZ"?

Spitz is the German for "spike" or "sharp point" (cognate with the English *spit,* which is a narrow headland or the sharp-pointed rod on which a roast is rotated over the fire). It seems that the dogs—popular as guard dogs in Germany and Scandinavia since the Dark Ages—were first described as *spitz* in the fifteenth century, most likely because of their sharp muzzles and pointed ears. The term is now applied to a number of similar breeds, none of which is otherwise of a "spiky" temperament or has peculiarly sharp claws.

P. G. WODEHOUSE ON COMIC DOGS

"It is fatal to let any dog know that he is funny,
for he immediately loses his head and starts hamming it up."
P. G. WODEHOUSE (1881–1975) *British humorist and novelist*

CANIS SAPIENS

An oft-cited but totally informal (i.e., non-scientific)
list of dogs supposedly in rank order of intelligence:

1. . . . . *Border collie*	6. . . . . *Shetland sheepdog*
2. . . . . *Poodle*	7. . . . . *Labrador*
3. . . . . *German shepherd*	8. *Papillon*
4. . . . .*Golden retriever*	9. . . . . *Rottweiler*
5. . . . .*Doberman(n) pinscher*	10. . . . . *Australian cattle dog*

PICASSO'S DOG

The most famous piece of art by Pablo Picasso (1881–1973) that features a
dog (generally known just as *The Dog*) is a simple but clever line-drawing of
a dachshund, Lump, that is now available in the form of a poster. However,
Lump (the name is English because the dog originally belonged to an American
photojournalist friend) also features in 15 of the series of 44 paintings by Picasso
collectively called *Las Meninas* (after a painting by Velázquez) now in the
Picasso Museum, Barcelona. Having lived with Picasso for 16 years, Lump
died exactly a week before the artist himself did.

BEAGLE AIRCRAFT

BEAGLE AIRCRAFT was formed in 1962 through the
merger of the British Pressed Steel Company's aircraft
design department (formerly British Executive and General
Aviation Ltd., or BEAGLE) with aircraft manufacturers

Auster Aircraft and F. G. Miles Ltd. Within 4 years, however, Pressed Steel
had become part of the British Motor Corporation and no longer provided
backing funds or sponsored new designs. BEAGLE had to seek financial help from
the government, which initially responded by taking over the company, but
then—when finances continued to be a problem—called in the receivers. The
company was then (in 1969) split up and its assets sold off piece by piece.

In the meantime, the company had produced a number of aircraft of high
quality and excellent reputation. They included:

* the *Beagle Husky*—a single-engine, 3-seater light aircraft
* the *Beagle Terrier* and *Airedale*—single-engine, high-winged monoplanes
* the *Beagle Basset*—a twin-engine, low-winged light transport plane
* the *Beagle Pup*—a single-engine, low-winged, two-seater light aircraft

Some of these aircraft are still flying very successfully today.

DOG BLOOD GROUPS

Canine blood groups are categorized within the Dog Erythrocyte Antigen (DEA) system, although the total number of groups recognized in different countries varies between 10 and 13. All dogs belong to more than one group anyway (compare the human AB blood group), many to more than two. Moreover, individual dogs can be either positive or negative in any blood group other than DEA group 1, which comprises 3 subgroups in which a dog may be positive in one subgroup but negative in another. Perhaps it is just as well that dogs seem to have no naturally occurring antibodies to blood groups other than their own—which means that tissue-typing and cross-matching blood for a transfusion is usually unnecessary unless it is a second or later transfusion, or the dog is pregnant or likely to be. The concept of a "universal donor" blood group (like O-negative in humans) is therefore hardly relevant, although DEA groups 1.1-negative and 1.2-negative may be considered as such.

THE JOYS OF PARENTHOOD

"[My husband and I had] begun to long for the pitter-patter of little feet. So we bought a dog. Well, it's cheaper, and you get more feet."
RITA RUDNER (b. 1953) *U.S. comedienne, actress, and humorous writer*

THE MOLOSSUS: AN EXTINCT BREED

THE MOLOSSUS was a fierce animal with characteristics both of greyhounds and of mastiffs that was initially bred by the ancient Greek Molossian shepherds of Epirus to guard their flocks. The dogs gradually became heavier and more mastiff-like as the Hellenic people spread through the Balkans and into Italy. By the time the Romans were in control of the area, they were used both for hunting (as the classic *canes venatici*, commemorated as a constellation in the night sky) and as formidable protectors of the household.

The molossus is considered the ancestor of many of today's mastiff-type dogs, including the Saint Bernard and the Bernese mountain dog: these and similar dogs are sometimes referred to as "molossus dogs" or "molossers."

ONCE BITTEN!

Unlike cats, dogs do remember foods that make them feel unwell, and they tend to avoid them thereafter.

WHY DOGS LICK THEIR WOUNDS

It is often said that dogs lick their wounds because their saliva contains healing enzymes that also soothe and clean. Indeed, it has been scientifically proved that dogs' saliva contains healing enzymes, and it is fairly obvious that licking ought to do something toward cleaning a wound. Yet it is also a fact that the proportion of healing enzymes in dogs' saliva is actually rather small, that there is little means other than by licking a wound that a dog can treat itself in any way and so make itself feel better, and that far from always cleaning a wound, a dog's licking may abrade the edges of the wound and make it worse, even to the point of turning it septic.

AESOP'S FABLE: A MAN'S TWO DOGS

A MAN HAS TWO DOGS, one to go hunting with and one as a pet. The dog that is the hunter is jealous of having to work for his food and reward and remonstrates with the pet dog—but the pet dog says, "Don't blame me, blame the master. Children cannot be blamed for the faults of the parents."

LEFT- OR RIGHT-PAWED

Dogs are known to use one forepaw in preference to the other when initiating movement or activity. Most male dogs seem to be left-pawed, whereas a smaller majority of female dogs appear to be right-pawed.

THE SPORT OF FLYBALL

Flyball is a race for teams of 4 dogs who, one after another, hurdle 4 small jumps 10 feet (3 meters) apart, tap a spring-loaded panel on the "flyball box" at the far end that delivers a tennis ball, catch the ball, and return over the jumps to the starting line. Heats are run between two teams over parallel courses; the first team to finish wins the heat. There are penalties for dropping the ball or for any dog who begins before the preceding dog has fully crossed the starting line. Dogs can be any type or size: the jump height is adjusted to the shoulder height of the smallest dog in the team.

The first flyball tournament was held in 1983 in the United States. The European flyball championships were held in the United Kingdom in 2007 and in the Czech Republic in 2008. Most competitions are two-day weekend events. In March 2008, a team in a competition in Hurricane, Utah, completed the course (all 4 dogs) in 15.21 seconds.

— BEAGLE / PEKINGESE CROSSBREEDS / HYBRIDS —

Each has 12 named crossbreeds:

a Beagle &
a Bearded collie = a Beacol
a Bichon frise = a Glechon
a Boston terrier = a Boglen (terrier)
a Boxer = a Bogle
a Brussels griffon = a Bea griffon
a Cocker spaniel = a Bocker
a Dachshund = a Doxle
a Golden retriever = a Beago
a Jack Russell terrier = a Jack-a-bee
a Labrador = a Labbe
a Pekingese = a Peagle
a Pug = a Puggle

a Pekingese &
an American bulldog = a Bullnese
a Beagle = a Peagle
a Bichon frise = a Peke-a-chon
a Boston terrier = a Bostinese
a Chihuahua = a Cheeks
a Cocker spaniel = a Cockinese
a Maltese = a Peke-a-tese
a Papillon = a Peke-a-pap
a Pomeranian = a Pominese
a Pug = a Puginese
a Shih Tzu = a Shinese
a Yorkshire terrier = a Yorkinese

— ORIGIN OF "CHENILLE" —

Chenille is a French word that has been borrowed in many European languages and refers to a trimming on stately robes and fine dresses in the form of a velvety cord from which strands of wool or silk hang fairly loosely. But it got this meaning through being used as slang, for in eighteenth-century French, *chenille* was a term for a particularly hairy caterpillar. Even this, though, was figurative usage, for the word derives ultimately from the Latin *canicula*, "little (female) dog."

— CANINE SPIRIT BEINGS —

Although the Mexican and Spanish Central American legend is about El Cadejo, it seems that there are either two *cadejos* or perhaps two types of *cadejo*. The white *cadejo* protects travelers from harm at night, whereas the black *cadejo* actively seeks to injure and possibly kill travelers at night. Both appear in the form of a bull-sized shaggy dog with burning eyes. And although they are regarded as spirit beings, they are associated with a strong smell of goats and a high-pitched whistling sound. The black *cadejo*—which may be a form of the devil himself—has all the rapacity of a ravening wolf, rending and tearing its victims if the white *cadejo* is not near by.

It may be highly relevant to note that *cadejo* is also the local term for a mastiff-sized member of the weasel family, otherwise called a *tayra*.

-------- PROOF OF IDENTITY: THE NOSE PRINT --------

A dog's nose print is as unique as a human's fingerprints and, similarly, can be used for the purposes of accurate identification.

In Canada, a registry of dog nose prints has been kept since 1938 as a system for differentiating between dogs and providing proof of identity.

-------- POPULAR SCANDINAVIAN DOG NAMES --------

Popular dog names in 2005, in alphabetical order:

in Sweden		*in Finland*		*in Norway*
Bamse	Harn	Ilkka	Peni	Baldur
Bor	Hjördis	Kaira	Pilkku	Heldig
Bragi	Nanna	Kettu	Pomo	Lys
Einar	Odd	Lahja	Pyry	Ragnar
Flicka	Sif	Lumikki	Rekku	Sedna
Freya	Sigun	Manu	Sampo	Sven
Frigg	Skuld	Musti	Susi	
Gösta	Ulfig	Nalle	Varpu	
Gullveig	Vili	Nipsu	Viiru	
Gunn		Onni		

DOG JACKET SIZES

Dog jacket sizes, as measured and described, vary slightly between manufacturers, so the measurements below must be understood as averages only. Potential purchasers are advised to regard the chest measurements as the most important for fit. The length measurements should never be too short; a length that is too long can be adapted or shortened.

SIZE	CHEST	LENGTH
Small (S)	up to 13 in (33 cm)	8–10 in (20–25 cm)
Medium (M)	13½–15 in (34–38 cm)	10–12 in (25–30 cm)
Large (L)	15½–17 in (39–43 cm)	12–14 in (30–35 cm)
Extra-large (XL)	17½–19 in (44–48 cm)	14–16 in (35–40 cm)

MLAMBONJA

Mlambonja is Zulu for "hungry dog" and the name of a mountain, a mountain pass, two rivers, and a wilderness area in which hardy tourists enjoy hiking in the Drakensberg mountains of KwaZulu/Natal, South Africa. The wilderness area has World Heritage status.

FOODS FOR DOGS TO AVOID

✳ *chocolate in quantity*	theobromine content may be fatal to a dog, affecting the central nervous system and heart
✳ *onion/onion powder, garlic*	can cause canine anemia
✳ *thin bones from fish or poultry*	can be swallowed whole and cause obstruction or damage
✳ *cat food*	contains high amounts of fats and proteins unsuited to dogs' digestion
✳ *grapes & raisins*	contain a toxin apparently harmless to humans
✳ *mushrooms*	can be toxic to various canine organs
✳ *raw eggs*	contain avidin, which restricts absorption of the vitamin B biotin; can contain salmonella
✳ *coffee & tea*	contain caffeine, which affects the heart and nervous system and can be toxic to dogs

WHY DO DOGS WAG THEIR TAILS?

Dogs wag their tails to communicate. When they are alone, they do not wag their tails no matter how they are feeling. So the wagging of a tail is the delivering of information and is certainly not the simple radiating of enjoyment that many people suppose it to be. Very often, in the presence of a human, a wagging tail is a conscious expression of gratitude—for attention, for food, or for an anticipated pleasure. But if the tail is held high and only its tip is wagging, the dog may instead be indicating that it feels it has reason to be aggressive: many people have wondered why they have been bitten by a dog that seemed to be wagging its tail, without realizing that the wagging was different and they had been warned in advance.

U.S. GREYHOUND BETTING TERMS

Bets can be placed on a dog to win, to place (to come first or second), or to show (to come first, second, or third); a bet "across the board" is a simultaneous bet on all 3 of these options. A "quiniela" is a bet on two specified dogs to come first and second in either order; a "perfecta" is a bet on two dogs to come first and second in a specified order; a "trifecta" is a bet on 3 dogs to come first, second, and third in a specified order. A "daily double" is a bet on two specified dogs winning two races in a row at one meeting, whereas a "pick 6" is a bet on 6 specified dogs winning 6 races one after the other at one meeting.

SEGOVIA, ON MAN'S BEST FRIEND

"Among God's creatures, two—the dog and the guitar—
have taken all the sizes and all the shapes,
in order not to be separated from the man."
ANDRÉS SEGOVIA (1893–1987) *Spanish guitar virtuoso*

AESOP'S FABLE: THE DOGS & THE LION

A pack of dogs is traveling homeward through an area of rough grassland. Suddenly they see what looks like a lion asleep on the path ahead of them. They approach very cautiously, but discover that although it is a lion, it is not asleep but dead, and that other scavengers have already removed anything worth eating. So they tear the lion skin to pieces. A passing fox notes that if the lion had been alive, it would have been the dogs who were torn to pieces. The moral is that it is all too easy to kick a man who is already down.

DADDY WOULDN'T BUY ME A BOW-WOW

This famous British music hall song was written apparently in just a few minutes by Joseph Tabrar (1857–1931) in 1892—the same year that two other still well-known music hall songs achieved a greater popularity: "Daisy, Daisy" (properly, "Daisy Bell") by Harry Dacre, and "My Old Dutch" by Albert Chevalier and Charles Ingle. "Daddy Wouldn't Buy Me a Bow-Wow" was made famous by singer Vesta Victoria in the United Kingdom, but was associated much more in continental Europe with Irish entertainer May Belfort, after she was painted singing it in costume by Toulouse-Lautrec in Paris, France, in 1895.

1.

I love my little cat, I do,
    With soft black silky hair.
It comes with me each day to school
    And sits upon the chair.
When teacher says "Why do
    you bring
That little pet of yours?"
    I tell her that I bring my cat
Along with me because . . .

Chorus

Daddy wouldn't buy me a bow-wow!
    bow wow!
Daddy wouldn't buy me a bow-wow!
    bow wow!
I've got a little cat, and I'm very
    fond of that,
But I'd rather have a bow wow wow!

2.

We used to have two tiny dogs—
    Such pretty little dears—
But daddy sold 'em 'cause they used
    To bite each other's ears.
I cried all day. At 8 each night
    Papa sent me to bed.
When Ma came home and wiped
    my eyes,
I cried again and said . . .

Chorus

Daddy wouldn't buy me a bow-wow!
    bow wow!
Daddy wouldn't buy me a bow-wow!
    bow wow!
I've got a little cat, and I'm very
    fond of that,
But I'd rather have a bow wow wow!

3.

I'll be so glad, when I gets old,
    To do just as I likes.
I'll keep a parrot and at least
    A half a dozen tykes.
And when I've got a tiny pet,
    I'll kiss the little thing,
Then put it in its little cot
    And to it I will sing . . .

Chorus

Daddy wouldn't buy me a bow-wow!
    bow wow!
Daddy wouldn't buy me a bow-wow!
    bow wow!
I've got a little cat, and I'm very
    fond of that,
But I'd rather have a bow wow wow!

LADY & THE TRAMP

Disney's first animated movie in CinemaScope®, *Lady and the Tramp*, was based partly on a short story by Ward Greene in the 1940s called "Happy Dan, the Whistling Dog," whose main character became the film's scapegrace hero, the mongrel Tramp. The film's sympathetic heroine, the cocker spaniel from the respectable side of town, noble protectress of the infant of the human family to which she is devoted, was added by the Disney studio and may or may not have been named Lady after Walt Disney's own household pet. Featuring the voices of Barbara Luddy (Lady), Larry Roberts (Tramp), and Peggy Lee (several other animals), the movie premiered in mid-June 1955 and was rereleased in 1962, 1971, 1980, and 1986 (running time: 75 minutes). It has been available on video since 1987, and on DVD since 2006.

AQUATIC SPORT FOR DOGS

The sport of dock diving utilizes the well-attested love dogs have for jumping into water. For the event, each dog runs the length of a quayside (the "dock") and leaps off the end. The objective is to achieve distance ("Big Air") before hitting the water. The dog then turns and dog-paddles back to scramble out of the water up a gentle ramp at the side of the quay. Events may be divided into classes for different sizes and types of dog. Newcomers and nervous dogs may require practice jumps before their event jump, sometimes demanding considerable patience from other more accustomed competitors ("splash dogs") and their handlers. Safety personnel are always on duty.

POPULAR AMERICAN DOG NAMES

Most popular names for dogs in the United States in 2006:

MALE		FEMALE	
1. . . . . *Max*	11 . . . . . *Charlie*	1 . . . . . . *Maggie*	11 . . . . . . *Dakota*
2. . . . . *Jake*	12 . . . . *Jack*	2 . . . . *Molly*	12 . . . . *Katie*
3. . . . . . . *Buddy*	13 . . . . . *Harley*	3 . . . . *Lady*	13 . . . . . . *Annie*
4. . . . . . . *Bailey*	14 . . . . . . *Rusty*	4 . . . . . . *Sadie*	14 . . . . . . *Chelsea*
5. . . . . *Sam*	15 . . . . . . *Toby*	5 . . . . *Lucy*	15 . . . . . . *Princess*
6. . . . . . . *Rocky*	16 . . . . . *Murphy*	6 . . . . . . *Daisy*	16 . . . . *Missy*
7. . . . . . . *Buster*	17 . . . . . . *Shelby*	7 . . . . . . *Ginger*	17 . . . . . . *Sophie*
8. . . . . . . *Casey*	18 . . . . . *Sparky*	8 . . . . . . *Abby*	18 . . . . *Bo*
9. . . . . . . *Cody*	19 . . . . . *Barney*	9 . . . . . . *Sasha*	19 . . . . *Coco*
10. . . . . . *Duke*	20 . . . . . *Winston*	10 . . . . . *Sandy*	20 . . . . . . *Tasha*

SHAKESPEARE'S DOGS

SHAKESPEARE certainly did not avoid mentioning dogs in his plays—there are some very well-known quotations ("Cry Havoc! and let slip the dogs of war . . . ") among the 151 times he actually used the word "dog" in singular or plural. Moreover, it was not only the word "dog" he used with figurative or pejorative meanings. In *King Lear*, Kent describes Oswald as "the Sonne and Heire of a Mungrill Bitch" together with other less than complimentary epithets. But in only one of his plays does a dog actually make a physical entrance (Act II, Scene 2; Act IV, Scene 4) and become a "character" in a romantic subplot. That play is *The Two Gentlemen of Verona* (*c.* 1594), and the dog is Crab, quite unfairly described by its erratic master, Launce, servant to Proteus (one of the Two Gentlemen), as "the sourest-natured dog that lives . . . this cruel-hearted cur . . . a very pebble stone."

WOLVES & WOLFRAM

Wolfram is the old Germanic term for the metal now better known worldwide as "tungsten" (which is actually Swedish for "heavy stone"). But even when called tungsten, its technical abbreviation is W, standing for *wolfram*—a name of two word-elements, of which the first is agreed by all etymologists to be genuinely "wolf." Some of the theories concerning the second element (and published in highly respected dictionaries) have been distinctly bizarre, but perhaps the most believable theory is the notion that *wolfram* derives initially from Middle High German *Wolf-rumb*, or "wolf-turnip," because the metal is found naturally as a mineral (wolframite) in the form of turnip-sized lumps that have sharp edges like teeth.

DR. WHO'S DOG, K-9

K-9 (often wrongly spelled K9) is the robotic dog featured in the long-running British space-and-time TV series *Dr. Who*, first seen in 1977 (when Tom Baker was the Doctor), off the air between 1981 and 2005, returning at that point (with David Tennant as the Doctor) and for the spin-off *The Sarah Jane Adventures* (which was supposedly aimed more at children). The name is of course based on the standard English pronunciation of "canine." K-9's voice was supplied throughout by voice actor John Leeson.

K-9 was initially created by *Dr. Who* screenwriters Bob Baker and Dave Martin in 1977 at a time when Martin's own dog had recently been tragically run over, and he was thinking of a preferably permanent and indestructible canine replacement.

DAVID HOCKNEY & DOGS

The renowned English artist and photomontageur David Hockney (b. 1937) is not particularly well known for images of dogs in his work, but in 1998 he published a short book containing many paintings of his two dachshunds, Stanley and Boodgie. Hockney also wrote the accompanying text, in which he described the dogs as his "closest friends."

WHY DO DOGS BURY BONES?

Dogs bury bones because in the wild the bones are the last parts left after the pack has feasted on a carcass and is sated with meat. Dogs seem to be aware that bones do not decay as meat does, and may also contain nutrient-rich marrow, and so are worth storing. The bones can be carried back from the site of the kill to the pack lair, where dogs can chew on them from time to time if necessary, especially when kills are rare. It is part of the scavenging way of life, and dogs' dentition has evolved for it. Bones are not so much buried as put in a safe place that can be easily remembered—and if they do rot or become inedible, a dog will detect that soon enough by smell.

USES OF BULLDOG COTTON

Betsy Ross of Philadelphia, a friend of George Washington, sewed the first flag for what was to become the United States of America on June 14, 1777. It was made out of bulldog cotton, and the colors she used were "white for purity, red for hardiness and valour, and blue for vigilance, perserverance, and justice." Today, "Bulldog" U.S. flags are still made of bulldog cotton bunting, regarded as particularly strong, long-lasting, and color-retentive. Bulldog cotton is used also to make shorts, finger puppets, and various other items that require hard-wearing but soft fabric.

DOG-SLEDDING COMMANDS

The classic commands "mushers" give their sled dogs:

hike: start running (a form of "Hie" = "Go!")
gee: turn right (effectively to turn away)
haw: turn left (effectively to turn toward)
stop *or* **whoa**

It is likely that the commands "gee" and "haw" (borrowed from the horse-riding fraternity) represent the derivation of the famous cowboy yell "Yee-ha!"

IS TAIL-WAGGING INSTINCTIVE?

It is not by instinct that dogs wag their tails—it is a learned behavior that they pick up as part of the initial socializing process when surrounded by their siblings as they are nursed by their mother. Most puppies learn what the tail signals are, and how to make them, by the age of 7 weeks, by which time there is a definite need to be able to communicate as an individual.

THE BLUE PAUL TERRIER: AN EXTINCT BREED

The Blue Paul terrier was a short-haired, square-headed pit dog not unlike a bulldog. It was first described in Scotland in the 1770s, where it was thought to have been introduced from North America, and where it was used as a fighting dog, particularly by Romany travelers. The terrier was re-introduced to the United States in the 1890s, but was then bred out/mongrelized.

CANINE THERAPY

Medical records suggest that heart-attack patients who own dogs tend to show a better-than-average chance of survival and recovery.

"LOVE ME, LOVE MY DOG"

This is a quotation that in English, and in several other European languages, is taken to mean that if you intend to love a person, you must also accept that person's "baggage"—any past history, present faults and idiosyncrasies, and future disabilities and disappointments. This is not the meaning that the expression's originator had in mind. Saint Bernard of Clairvaux, in 1150, used it in a treatise, in Latin, describing the love of God and the need to fulfill all the requirements (notably faith, self-discipline, and the doing of good works) to be sure of experiencing that love.

THE PERFECT PET

"I have a great dog. She's half Lab[rador], half Pit bull.
A good combination. Sure, she might bite off my leg—
but she'll bring it back to me."
JIMI CELESTE *U.S. comedian, actor, and photographer*

——— AESOP'S FABLE: THE WOLF & THE LAMB ———

A wolf encounters a lamb that has strayed alone far from the fold, but decides that he will talk to the lamb and find a reason that the newborn animal will understand and accept for the wolf's eating him up. So he says to the lamb, "Young sir, last year you insulted me unforgivably." "Actually," bleats the lamb sorrowfully, "I hadn't been born then." "In that case you have been eating grass in my meadow," says the wolf sternly. "No," says the lamb— "I have yet to try eating grass." "Then you have been drinking at my well," insists the wolf. "Not so, sir," replies the lamb, "for I have so far consumed only my mother's milk." Without further ado, the wolf ate the lamb anyway, saying to himself, "Well, I am not going to go without my dinner, for all your answers to my assertions." And the moral is that the tyrant will always find excuses for his tyrannical behavior.

——— CHIHUAHUA / PUG CROSSBREEDS / HYBRIDS ———

Each has 6 named crossbreeds:

a Chihuahua &	*a Pug &*
a Papillon = a Chion	*a Beagle* = a Puggle
a Pekingese = a Cheeks	*a Boston terrier* = a Bugg
a Pomeranian = a Chiranian	*a Chihuahua* = a Chug
a Pug = a Chug	*a Jack Russell terrier* = a Jug
a Shih Tzu = a ShiChi	*a West Highland terrier* = a Pugland
a Yorkshire terrier = a Chorkie	*a Yorkshire terrier* = a Pugshire

——— BIGGLES, THE FACE OF HUSH PUPPIES ———

The basset hound featured in the Hush Puppies shoe ads was named Biggles.

——————— EYE COLOR ———————

The genes that determine the color of a domestic dog's eyes are mainly those that are also responsible for the color of the dog's coat. The relatively few eye-coloration genes that are independent of coat-color genes generally affect only the intensity of color in the iris, although dogs that possess the merle coat-color gene may turn out to have eyes of two different colors or eyes that individually contain two different colors. Meanwhile, the irises of wild dogs—notably wolves—are generally much lighter-colored than those of the domestic dog.

QIQIRN: DOG SPIRIT OF THE INUIT

Qiqirn is a spirit being in Inuit mythology. It appears in the form of a huge dog that has hair only at its mouth and tail-tip and on its feet and ears, but is otherwise bald. It is frightening to behold—so much so that it may cause people who see it to lose consciousness and/or have convulsions—but it is itself timorous in the presence of humans, and particularly fearful of hearing its own name. (This makes continual repetition of its name a useful method of avoiding being confronted by it.)

ORIGIN OF THE WORD "KENNEL"

The name of the authoritative national dog association in many countries is a variant on the English words "kennel" and "club." Thus, for example, in Finland the Finnish Kennel Club is *Suomen Kenelliitto* (in which -*liitto* corresponds to "club") and in Swedish is *Finska Kennelklubben*. But even in English, *kennel* has no immediately obvious linguistic connection with dogs. Yet it is connected—historically, through Norman French, the language of the conquerors of England in 1066. When these lordly aristocrats set themselves up in their castles on their new estates all over England, they hired the local serfs—who spoke Anglo-Saxon—to do all the menial chores. Some in each castle were thus deputed to look after the pack of hunting dogs, which had its own special quarters somewhere behind the kitchens. To the Norman French nobles, the pack of dogs comprised *la canaille* (ultimately from the Latin diminutive plural *caniculi*, "little dogs"), but to the Anglo-Saxon peasants who looked after the dogs that word seemed to mean the place in which they worked and where the dogs were kept, and they adapted it over time to "the kennel."

MOST VETERINARY CARE

A survey, conducted in the United States in 2005, intended to establish which breeds of dog required the most veterinary care, based on the money spent on treatment over a single year. These statistics therefore take no account of the different numbers of each breed in the United States, nor of the general state of health of each breed. Neither do they take account of the fees charged by individual vets.

1. . . . . *Labrador*	6. *Irish setter*
2. . . . . *Bichon frise*	7. . . . . *Golden retriever*
3. . . . . *Chow*	8. . . . . *Basset hound*
4. . . . . *Dachshund*	9. . . . . *Cocker spaniel*
5. . . . . *Doberman(n)*	10. . . . . *Standard poodle*

TRACKING TRIALS

A tracking trial is a sporting competition in which a dog is required to follow a scent trail laid a short time earlier by a "tracklayer," and to pick up or alert a handler to various articles left along the trail by the tracklayer before finally finding the tracklayer in person at the end of the trail. The trail is then re-laid (and the articles replaced) for the next dog competitor. The degree of difficulty in the trails and the number of articles to be found differ according to the rules of the event's organizing authority and the anticipated skill of the competing dogs. Each dog is attached to its handler by a fairly lengthy lead (generally 30 feet [10 meters] unless the terrain is exceptionally rough), which must not be used to guide or encourage the dog in any directional sense. A successful trial leads to the award by the organizing authority of a "pass"; receipt of a specified number of passes in competition over time may in due course lead to the further award of a trophy or title to dog and handler.

·POPULAR DOG NAMES: FRANCE / GERMANY / ITALY·

Popular names, in alphabetical order, in 2005:

in France		*in Germany*		*in Italy*
Adèle	Etoile	Axel	Max	Bella
Alette	Gaspard	Berthe	Mercedes	Bimba
Angéline	Ignace	Blitzen	Pfötchen	Bosco
Barn	Lisette	Bodo	Rex	Cesare
Beau	Loulou	Elska	Schatzi	Chiara
Bébé	Malo	Eugen	Schnitzel	Fabio
Bison	Merlot	Falke	Ulla	Fausto
Catan	Milou	Grau	Uschi	Flavio
Céline	Mustache	Halma		Mauro
Cozette	Neige	Hansi		Pepe
Drogo	Toutou	Hiske		Tino

WHY *VIZSLA*?

Vizsla is often described as the Hungarian for "alert" or "ready to respond," but it would seem in fact either to be more closely related to words meaning "to examine" or to be an adaptation of a Turkish word originally meaning "to seek." In any case, the word is now solely used in Hungarian as the equivalent of "pointer" or "retriever."

DOG WHISTLES

The old-fashioned type, audible to humans and everything else for miles around.

*The modern so-called "silent" dog whistle —
except that dogs can hear it or there would be no point.*

*A modern plastic style of dog whistle,
really just a replacement for the old-fashioned type.*

*A plastic version of the classic sheepdog whistle that fits inside the
handler's mouth between the teeth. It requires a certain amount of practice
to use competently. And a certain number of teeth.*

CANADIAN TOWNSHIP NAMED AFTER DOG

The township of Tiny is located at the southernmost tip of Georgian Bay in Simcoe County, southern Ontario, Canada. It is in an area that is important archaeologically, as the traditional homeland of the Huron people, and for retaining both English and French cultural associations, although today it relies

mainly on tourism. The township was named Tiny by Lady Maitland, wife of the Lieutenant-Governor of Canada in the early 1800s, after one of her 3 lapdogs. The adjoining townships of Tay and Flos were named after the other two, although Flos has since been incorporated into Springwater.

DOCKING THE TAIL

The issue of docking remains controversial – proponents both for and against the whole notion of docking tails are emotively vociferous all over the world – although the legal situation as of 2008 is clear.

In Australia, South Africa, Scotland and most countries in continental Europe, the docking of dogs' tails is altogether banned. In England and Wales, the "cosmetic" docking of tails is banned, but the docking of tails of working dogs for health and safety reasons is not banned.

In the United States, Canada, New Zealand, Northern Ireland, the Irish Republic, most countries of Central and South America, and one or two countries of continental Europe, the practice of docking (or "bobbing") is not banned but politicians and veterinary societies have put forward measures that suggest that in time a complete ban will be introduced. Breeders, vets, show dog owners, show judges, and any other interested parties should keep an eye out for developments.

MOST COMPANIONABLE DOGS

Not regarded by national Kennel Clubs as a group for the purposes of a dog show, there is nonetheless a fairly well-accepted list of dog breeds that are held to be particularly suitable to live with and accompany humans in daily life. These are known as "companion" dogs and are drawn mainly from the toy and non-sporting groups.

They include (in alphabetical order):

* *Basenji* . . . .
* *Bichon frise* . . . .
* *Bolognese (Bichon Bolognese)* . . . .
* *Cavalier King Charles spaniel* . . .
* *Chihuahua* . . . .
* *Chinese crested dog* . . . .
* *Coton de Tulear* . . . .
* *English bulldog* . . . .
* *German spitz*
  (giant, standard, small) . . . .
* *Havanese* . . . .
* *Inca hairless dog* . . . .
* *Italian greyhound* . . . .
* *Japanese Chin* . . . .
* *Japanese spitz* . . . .
* *Keeshond* . . . .
* *King Charles spaniel* . . . .

* *Kyi Leo* . . . .
* *Lhasa Apso* . . . .
* *Löwchen (little lion dog)* . . . .
* *Maltese* . . . .
* *Mexican hairless dog* . . . .
* *Papillon* . . . .
* *Pekingese* . . . .
* *Phalène (butterfly dog)* . . . .
* *Pomeranian* . . . .
* *Pug* . . . .
* *Shih Tzu* . . . .
* *Tibetan spaniel* . . . .
* *Tibetan terrier (Dhoki Apso)* . . . .
* *Toy American eskimo dog* . . . . . .
* *Toy/miniature poodle* . . . .
* *Volpino Italiano*
  (Cane de Quirinale) . . . .

RODRIGUE'S BLUE DOG

George Rodrigue is a U.S. painter (b. 1944) native to the Cajun area of the southern state of Louisiana. His early work consisted mainly of family portraits within a setting of oak trees and posters for the New Orleans Jazz Festival. Then his dog Tiffany died—and Rodrigue began including in his artworks a strangely stylized image of the dog, seated staring directly at the observer through round yellow eyes, its coat a vibrant blue color except for a white blaze around and above the nose. It has been suggested that the idea derived at least in part from the Cajun legend of the *loup-garou* (in which, remarkably, *garou* is in fact etymologically cognate with the English word "werewolf"), although Tiffany had evidently been some sort of terrier, and female. Rodrigue's blue dog was nonetheless from 1992 used very successfully in advertising material both for Absolut Vodka and for the Xerox Corporation, becoming so well known as to give rise to the expression "a Blue Dog Democrat," which refers to a particularly conservative member of the U.S. Democratic Party.

Following the 9/11 terrorist attacks in New York and Washington D.C., and then the destruction wrought in his home state by Hurricane Katrina in 2005, Rodrigue set up a Blue Dog Relief fund to assist victims and their families. By 2008, mostly through the sale of art prints Rodrigue had specially created, the fund had raised well over $2 million.

THE BLUE DOG OF CHARLES COUNTY

Somewhere on Rose Hill Road outside Port Tobacco (est. 1727; population 15 in 2000) in Charles County, Maryland, a quantity of gold together with the title deeds to a property lie buried and are watched over by the spirit of a large blue dog. The dog is the ghost of the animal who in life was the companion of Charles Sims, a soldier recently returned from fighting in the Revolutionary War (the American War of Independence, 1775–1783) and owner of both gold and property. Sims was treacherously killed for them, together with his dog, by one Henry Hanos who had "befriended" Sims in a tavern in the town. Hanos buried the "treasure" beside the road nearby, meaning to return to collect it once the dust of his crime had settled. When he attempted to do so, however, he was given such a fright by the ghost of the Blue Dog that he fled empty-handed and himself died before he could summon up enough nerve to go back again.

The last sighting of the Blue Dog was purportedly in 1897, when a local landowner reported to the *Port Tobacco Times* that she had seen it. Although that report is now more than a century old, residents of the area still insist that the Blue Dog remains on guard at his master's grave. And certainly, no one has ever publicly claimed to have unearthed the treasure.

TALLEST DOGS

The Irish wolfhound is the tallest dog breed, measured at the shoulders when standing on all four feet. However, currently listed as the world's tallest living dog in *The Guinness Book of World Records* (from August 2004) is Gibson, a Harlequin Great Dane resident of Grass Valley, California, whose shoulder height is 42⅛ in (107 cm), and who, when standing on his hind feet with his forepaws up against a wall or a on sturdy person's shoulders, is more than 7 feet (2.13 meters) tall.

MARK TWAIN & THE GRATEFUL DOG

"If you pick up a starving dog and make him prosperous, he will not bite you. This is the principal difference between a dog and a man."
MARK TWAIN (Samuel Clemens, 1835–1910)
U.S. novelist, journalist, and lecturer

101 DALMATIANS

The animated Disney movie *One Hundred and One Dalmatians* (1961; re-released 1969, 1979, 1985, and 1991 is based on the book (*The Hundred and One Dalmatians*, 1956) by Dodie Smith, in which the 15 puppies of dalmatians Pongo and Perdita are kidnapped by the wicked Cruella De Vil to add to her collection in order eventually to make a dogskin coat out of them. The rescue of Pongo and Perdita's 15 puppies plus another 84 puppies, and the return home of all 101, makes up the rest of the story. The animated Pongo has been cited as having 72 dalmatian spots, Perdita 68, and the pups 32 each. The live-action remake of the film in 1996, again by Disney, starred Glenn Close as Cruella De Vil and required various alterations in the storyline, chiefly so that none of the animals was required to speak. A sequel—*102 Dalmatians*—was released in 2000.

THE BULLENBEISSER: AN EXTINCT BREED

Also in English called the German Bulldog, the Bullenbeisser ("bull-biter") was a direct descendant of the short-haired working dog of Central Asia known as the Alaunt, which flourished in the early centuries CE. In the late nineteenth century, the Bullenbeisser became progenitor of the modern Boxer and Great Dane breeds (both of them German). However, by 1900 deliberate crossbreeding had made extinction of the purebreed Bullenbeisser inevitable.

THE DOG BOATS OF WORLD WAR II

The "dog boat" was the Fairmile D-class motor torpedo/gun boat designed to compete against German Schnellbooten and Italian MAS torpedo boats, anywhere from the North Sea through the English Channel and south to the Bay of Biscay between England and northern Europe during World War II. They were nicknamed "dog boats" primarily because of their blunt prow, which forced its way, bulldog-like, into the waves (just as Dutch trawlers of similar frontages in previous centuries had been called *doggers*). Each boat used 4 Packard 1,250-horsepower engines and achieved a disappointingly slow maximum speed of 32 knots (around 35 mph or 56 km/h); sole weapons on board other than handguns were two 21-in (53.5-cm) torpedo tubes. The crews numbered 30–32 men mostly aged 18–19 and many from Commonwealth countries. Dog boats gained a remarkable reputation for efficient and successful service in wartime operations.

POPULAR BRITISH DOG NAMES

Popular dog names, in alphabetical order, in 2005:

in England		*in Scotland*		*in Wales*
Basil	Mojo	Ailsa	Morag	Bran
Beefy	Monty	Angus	Moss	Bryn
Bullet	Pilot	Bonnie	Tam	Celert
Deefer★	Princess	Cap		Dylan
Duke	Rocket	Dougal		Emlyn
Gromit	Wembley	Fingal		Glyn/Glen
Jasper	Windsor	Laddie		Gwen
Jet	Winston	Mackenzie		Morgan
Kim	★ *as in "D for Dog"*	MacTavish		Rhian

WHY "PINSCHER"? WHY "TERRIER"?

If you look up "terrier" in an English-German or French-German dictionary, you will find it translated as *Pinscher*. And if you look up "Pinscher" in a German-English or German-French dictionary, you will find it translated as *terrier*. Yet the root meanings of both terms are utterly different. A Pinscher is literally a "nipper," a "biter"—cognate with English "pincher" and "pincer." A terrier, on the other hand, pursues creatures into their burrows under the earth—under the *terra*in and into their own *terri*tory—a chaser, not a biter.

—————— AESOP'S FABLE: THE HOUND & THE HARE ——————

A hound chases a hare and catches her several times over, sometimes biting her and sometimes instead licking her in apparent friendship and comfort.

The hare is not unnaturally resentful: "Are you friend or foe? No one can be a friend unless there is some degree of trust."

FEMALES DEADLIER THAN MALES ——————

Female dog bites are statistically twice as numerous as male dog bites.

————————— THE DOG TREADMILL —————————

The dog treadmill—for exercising dogs and keeping them in good shape (which is especially important for show dogs)—was first patented in the United States in 1939. Modern versions have a number of safety features, although the most important safety aspect of the purchase and use of a treadmill is to ensure that it is the correct size (specifically length) and power for the dog—pet treadmills are virtually all motorized.

The advantages are:
✳ the dog handler does not have to exercise at the same time or at the same rate as the dog, which means that elderly or infirm dog owners can exercise their dogs perfectly well.
✳ exercise takes place indoors, out of any inclement weather.
✳ there are far fewer potential distractions for the dog, who should also appreciate effectively closer personal attention from the handler.

The disadvantages are:
✳ training may be required for the dog to understand the purpose of the treadmill and to enjoy using it
✳ monitoring the dog on the treadmill may require more attention to its movements and reactions than when walking (or running) around the block or across the park.
✳ exercise on a treadmill is not a substitute for a normal walk.
✳ the dog may shed hair and drool over the treadmill, which will require regular maintenance.
✳ regular maintenance of the dog's claws will also be required to prevent holes in the treadmill belt.
✳ it is not practical to exercise more than one dog at a time.

RESEARCH INTO TAIL WAGGING

T he eyes of a dog are more sensitive to movement than they are to visual details such as shape or color. This is what makes a moving tail so important as a means of communication between one dog and another. Evolution has tended to emphasize it: many wild dogs have bushy tails that are specifically visible from a distance, and most domestic dogs have tails that feature some form of contrast in color and markings that may also accentuate the tail tip in such a way that even when the tail is not moving, the position in which it is held stationary is conspicuous. In 2007, Italian researchers at the University of Trieste further suggested that dogs wag their tail "to the right" when they see something familiar (such as their owner) and "to the left" when they see something unfamiliar and potentially threatening, although the directional bias is so slight as to be measurable only through calibrated video analysis.

ESKIMO DOG / BASSET HOUND HYBRIDS

Each has 4 named crossbreeds:

an American eskimo dog &	***a Basset hound &***
a Cocker spaniel = a Cockamo	*a Boston terrier* = a Basston
a Lhasa Apso = a Kimola	*a Dachshund* = a Basschshund
a Pomeranian = a Pomimo	*a Pug* = a Bassug(g)
a Shetland sheepdog = an Eskland	*a Shar Pei* = a Ba-Shar

THE HOUND OF THE BASKERVILLES

Possibly the most famous Sherlock Holmes story of all, *The Hound of the Baskervilles,* appeared first in serial form over 9 monthly issues of *The Strand* magazine between 1901 and 1902. The author, Arthur Conan Doyle, was at the time a country doctor based in Plymouth, Devon, on the edge of Dartmoor in southwest England, and he used that wild location as background in the story. He also incorporated elements of the local folklore concerning the yeth hound (or yell hound), a black dog thought to be the spirit of an unbaptized child that rambled and wailed across the bleak countryside at night. Conan Doyle's hound of the Baskervilles—representing the supposed curse on the Baskerville family—is accordingly "an enormous coal-black hound, but not such a hound as mortal eyes have ever seen."

Perhaps because of its supernatural connotations, *The Hound of the Baskervilles* had by 2008 been filmed (as a movie or for TV) around 30 times, predominantly in English (once in Australia, once in Canada) but also in German, Italian, and Russian.

──────── ANGULATION, GAIT & SOUNDNESS ────────

Three points judges look for in a dog at a dog show:
Angulation: *the angles at which limbs meet each other at the joints*
Gait: *the way the dog walks, trots, and runs; an easy flow of motion indicates both underlying structure and physical condition*
Soundness: *mental and physical well-being as present and demonstrated*

──────────── ALLERGIES IN DOGS ────────────

Dogs are subject to various allergies, which may be classified in 5 groups:

✳ *bacterial allergies* ✳ *food allergies* ✳ *contact allergies*
✳ *flea allergies* ✳ *inhalant allergies (atopy)*

Bacterial allergies generally cause lesions and/or patchy hair loss; they can be treated with antibiotics.

Food allergies, when serious, may cause respiratory distress, but otherwise may just cause digestive problems and itchy skin; treatment is avoidance of the allergenic food following diagnosis by a process of elimination.

Contact allergies, which may result from contact with plastic feeding bowls, wool bedding, unwashed shirts and sweaters, and rubbing flea collars, tend to cause swelling, red and itchy skin, and patchy hair loss; treatment is avoidance of the allergenic item following diagnosis by a process of elimination.

Flea allergies generally cause scratching, lesions, and patchy hair loss; treatment is to find out where the fleas are coming from and eliminate them (or remove the dog), and administer corticosteroids as prescribed by a vet.

Inhalant allergies result from swallowing dust particles, pollen, and molds and cause continuous scratching and symptoms that in humans would be described as having a heavy cold; treatment requires diagnosis by a vet and may then include prescribed antihistamines and/or corticosteroids and dietary supplements; the environment in the home should be reassessed and if necessary humidifiers and air filters introduced.

──────────── THE NUMERATE DOG ────────────

"If you think dogs can't count, try putting 3 dog biscuits
in your pocket and then giving Fido only two of them."
PHIL PASTORET *U.S. humorous writer*

THE KURI: AN EXTINCT BREED

The kuri was the mid-sized dog introduced to New Zealand by the Maori on their arrival there from the Polynesian islands. It had a smallish head like a terrier but had exceptionally powerful jaws suitable for gnawing the bones of fur seals, moas, and pilot whales that formed the main diet of its human guardians. Although in times of scarcity the kuri might itself be used as a source of emergency food by those guardians, at other times the relationship was close enough for some kuri to be buried alongside humans. The purebreed dog became extinct shortly after the arrival of European settlers in New Zealand, although feral crossbreeds roamed the outback of the South Island until the late nineteenth century.

LET SLEEPING DOGS LIE

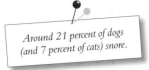

Around 21 percent of dogs (and 7 percent of cats) snore.

POLICE DOGS: RECRUITMENT & TRAINING

The typical police dog in Europe, North America, and elsewhere is assessed for acceptance at the age of about 12 months. Acceptance depends on size (preferably around 23 in [58.5 cm] tall at the shoulder) and temperament (neither agressive nor timorous, too bold or too friendly). If accepted, the dog undergoes 8 weeks' training in obedience, agility, retrieval, and tracking, with further schooling in how to chase and detain criminals. The dog is then licensed to work with its handler for 12 months at a time and reviewed every year. Each dog normally lives with its handler but may spend time in police kennels when necessary. A police dog generally retires after 6 or 7 years' work, although it may enjoy an active work life for at least 3 more years. The most popular police dog worldwide is the German shepherd.

PULKKA & ITS ASSOCIATED SPORT

Outside Scandinavia, pulkka (or pulka or pulk) in connection with dogs is the sport of harnessing a small low-running sled, now generally made of solid plastic, to one or two dogs for it/them to pull a weight, a child, or an adult over a measured distance of flat snow while being timed. In Scandinavia, the *pulkka* (Finnish), *pulka* (Swedish), or *pulk* (Norwegian) is the sled itself, so called as an adaptation of a *Lapp* (Saami) word.

THE DOG AS EVOLVED MAMMAL

The Canidae emerged from the Arctoidea who themselves evolved from the Creodonts, primitive carnivores that lived alongside the last of the dinosaurs.

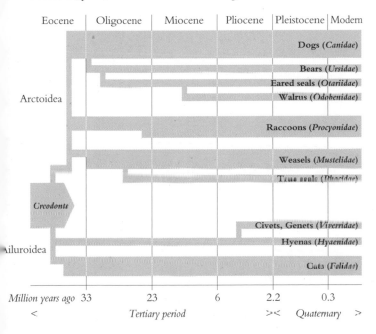

Eocene	Oligocene	Miocene	Pliocene	Pleistocene	Modern

Dogs (*Canidae*)

Bears (*Ursidae*)

Eared seals (*Otariidae*)

Walrus (*Odobenidae*)

Arctoidea

Raccoons (*Procyonidae*)

Weasels (*Mustelidae*)

True seals (*Phocidae*)

Creodonts

Civets, Genets (*Viverridae*)

Hyenas (*Hyaenidae*)

Ailuroidea

Cats (*Felidae*)

Million years ago   33   23   6   2.2   0.3

<   Tertiary period   ><   Quaternary   >

HAIR OF THE DOG

Based on the medieval European concept that like cures like—reflected in the myth that the best cure for a dog bite is to put a hair of the same dog on the wound—the ordinary meaning of this expression in English is the attempt to cure a hangover by consuming some more alcohol. Scientific research (mostly by unnamed researchers) has proved that it works . . . for a short time. The dehydrated hungover body—trying to eliminate the alcohol—enjoys the fluid intake and suspends alcohol elimination, so the patient feels better. But at a certain point the hangover will start again, and it will now last longer because of the increased presence of alcohol. Imbibing the "hair of the dog" is thus simply delaying the inevitable, and the overall effect is anything but a cure—with a possible tendency to increase the likelihood of alcohol addiction.

—————— WHY "KEESHOND"? ——————

The Keeshond is also known by the much more descriptive name of "Wolf spitz"—and it was because of its spitz-type characteristics (the dog was used particularly as a protector and companion on Dutch canal boats) that during the last decades of the eighteenth century it somewhat ironically became known instead as the Keeshond. This was the era of the French Revolution, when across north-western Europe aristocrats trembled and the lower classes flexed their new-found political muscle. In Holland, the leader of "the Patriots"—a group of lower- and lower-middle-class citizens that mounted a forceful and partly successful challenge to the ruling royal House of Orange—was one Cornelis de Gyselaer. The usual pet form of the name Cornelis in Holland is Kees (pronounced like the English word "case"), and de Gyselaer not only called his own Wolf spitz dog Kees after himself, but made the image of the animal a symbol and mascot of his political subgroup. Once the image of the dog was fixed with that special meaning in people's minds, any other of the same breed was then called a Kees dog, or *Kees-hond* in Dutch.

—————— HOUNDING BY SIGHT OR SCENT ——————

Hounds can be divided into sight hounds—who follow the prey by sight—and scent hounds—who track the prey by scent.

SCENT HOUNDS		SIGHT HOUNDS
Alpine dachsbracke	English coonhound	Afghan hound
American black & tan	English foxhound	Azawakh
coonhound	Estonian hound	Basenji
American foxhound	Finnish hound	Borzoi
Ariegeois	Griffon fauve	Canaan dog
Basset hound	Hanoverian hound	Carolina dog
Bavarian mountain dog	Harrier	Chart Polski
Beagle	Otterhound	Greyhound
Black Forest hound	Plott hound	Ibizan hound
Bloodhound	Poitevin	Irish wolfhound
Bluetick coonhound	Polish hound	Italian greyhound
Briquet Griffon Vendéen	Porcelaine	New Guinea singing dog
Chien d'Artois	Redbone coonhound	Rhodesian ridgeback
Chien Français	Spanish hound	Saluki
Dachshund	Treeing Walker coonhound	Scottish deerhound
Deutsche bracke		Sloughi
Drever		Whippet
Dunker		Xoloitzcuintli

GEORGE ELIOT ON DOGS

"Agreeable friends, [dogs] ask no questions; they pass no criticisms."
GEORGE ELIOT (Mary Anne Evans, 1819–1880) *English novelist*

THE ETYMOLOGICAL WOLF

It would seem that the original meaning behind the Indo-European root form was descriptive of the animal perhaps as a "tearer" or "ripper," and that the word could apply equally therefore both to the wolf and to the fox.

Indo-European root *★wulqos/★wulkw*

Lithuanian *vilkas* "wolf"	**Gothic** *wulfs* "wolf"	**Latin** *uulpes* "fox"
	Old English *wulf*	(English *vulpine*)
	German *Wolf*	
	English *wolf*	
	Danish *ulv*	
ancient Greek *lykos* "wolf"		**ancient Greek** *alōpex* "fox"
		Latin *lupus* "wolf"
		Spanish *lobo* "wolf"
		French *loup* "wolf"

DREAMING DOGS

Dogs can certainly dream—as is evident when watching the rippling eyelids of a sleeping dog (the equivalent of rippling eyelids in humans during rapid-eye-movement or dreaming sleep). This implies the recreation of past events in the dogs' minds and a continuity of "narration" in the scenario of the dream—both of which were once thought beyond dogs' capability.

DOG GUARDIAN OF THE UNDERWORLD

Surma—which means "slaughter" in Finnish—is a huge dog with a snake-like tail who stands guard at the gates of the Underworld (Tuonela) in the Finnish national epic *Kalevala*. Like many such protectors in mythology worldwide (notably dragons, Gorgons, and so forth), it is Surma's eyes that are most potent and can petrify those who meet its stare.

The English word "harm" may or may not be linguistically akin to the Finnish *surma*; the English words "sore" and "sorrow" (which have many Germanic cognates) undoubtedly are.

―――――TONGUE COLORS & CHOW ANCESTRY―――――

Black spots or streaks on a dog's tongue are occasionally said to indicate chow ancestry (since chows have black tongues), especially in a dog with spitz characteristics. This is, however, genetically untrue. In fact, it is comparatively common for *any* breed of dog to have odd patches of black pigmentation on the tongue as a sort of birthmark. Conversely, a dog that looks like a chow but has a pink tongue is unlikely in fact to have much in the way of chow ancestry (it is certainly not a purebreed chow) by at least 3 generations, but will almost definitely turn out to be the crossbreed product of two other spitz-type dogs.

――――――――― BARKING SANDS, HAWAII ―――――――――

BARKING SANDS Beach on the Hawaiian island of Kauai was apparently so named because of the sound made by its coarse, dry sand when trodden underfoot— a sort of "yap" or squeaky bark. Today, however, few people get to experience the beach's auditory qualities because the area has been taken over by the United States military authorities, specifically the Pacific Missile Range Facility Hawaiian Area (PACMISRANFAC HAWAREA for short). Local residents continue to call it Barking Sands— only now they may just possibly have in mind the mental condition of those who prevent them from visiting it despite a state law guaranteeing free public access to all beaches.

―――― HOW THE NAME "ROVER" BECAME POPULAR ――――

Rescued by Rover was a highly successful and cinematographically advanced film released in Britain in 1905. Lasting 6 minutes, it presented the story of how a kidnapped baby was recovered by the canny household dog (played by producer Cecil Hepworth's own dog, actually called Blair). The name Rover, relatively uncommon until then, thereafter became popular.

――――――――――― LARGEST DOG BISCUIT ―――――――――――

The largest dog biscuit so far ever made was baked by the People's Company Bakery in Minneapolis, Minnesota, on behalf of Mary Jo Johnson of Animal Ark (the publishing company), to whom it was presented on August 11, 1999. Rectangular in shape but with rounded edges, the biscuit measured 7 feet 8½ in (2.35 m) by 1 foot 10½ in (57 cm), and was 1 in (2.54 cm) thick.

——ST. JOHN'S WATER DOG: AN EXTINCT BREED——

The St. John's water dog was a sturdy medium-sized dog not unlike a dark-colored English Labrador. It had characteristic patches of white coloration on its muzzle, chin, chest, and feet, making it look as if it was wearing a tuxedo. The early history of the breed remains unknown, however. It was certainly resident among the fisherfolk of Newfoundland (of which the city of St. John's is the capital and chief port) before 1800, and large numbers of the dogs were exported from there to Britain between then and 1910 (where they were crossbred with other dogs, contributing significantly to the derivation of most of today's retrievers, including the Golden retriever and the Labrador, individuals of which may even now display vestiges of the white markings described above). The extinction of the breed by about 1915 came about partly through a heavy tax on dog ownership levied in Newfoundland in order to encourage sheep farming, and partly because of the collapse of the export market following strict quarantine measures initially established in Britain in 1885 to prevent the spread of rabies.

——TOP DOG NAMES: AUSTRALIA / NEW ZEALAND——

Popular names, in alphabetical order, in 2005:

in Australia				*in New Zealand*	
✳ Billy	✳ Cheezel	✳ Kylie		✳ Ayla	✳ Kea
✳ Bitzer	✳ Dingo	✳ Mate		✳ Baz	✳ Kiri
✳ Bladder	✳ Frizzle	✳ Pepper		✳ Fluke	✳ Prince
✳ Blue(y)	✳ Gumby	✳ Taz		✳ Jess	✳ Rocks
✳ Bowser	✳ Kira	✳ Toohey		✳ Jonah	✳ Tracey

——————LONGEST EARS——————

In 2004, the ears of basset hound Mr. Jeffries (more formally known in pedigree contexts as Knightsfollie Ladiesman) were officially recorded in the *Guinness Book of World Records* as 11½ in (29.2 cm) long. To some extent the ears were the bane of his life: he kept tripping over them as he walked and frequently failed to avoid trailing them through the food in his dog bowl. Yet he found fame, and his owner—Philip Jeffries, of West Sussex, England—found some fortune, in having his aural appendages photographed for diverse publications as the longest in the world.

At the same time, it meant that the ears had to be insured for no less than £25,000 (or $48,000 at contemporary exchange rates).

THE REMARKABLE LUNDEHUND

THE LUNDEHUND ("puffin dog" in Norwegian) has 6 (sometimes more) toes on each foot, extra joints for flexibility, and can close its ears shut tight. It was specially bred to scale rocky cliffs in Norway in order to catch and bring back tasty puffins for its owner to eat. The ability to close its ears was essential both if it fell off a cliff into water and if hit by a blast of air when down a draughty burrow. But as the human demand for puffin meat declined, so did the overall numbers of the dog, until at one point only 50 individuals were known to exist.

GOOFY: FILM & TV CAREER

It is hard to tell, but the Disney animated character Goofy—friend and associate of Mickey Mouse, Donald Duck, and others—is meant to be a bloodhound. He first appeared in the short movie *Mickey's Revue* in 1932, although in that and in a few subsequent shorts he was actually called Dippy Dawg. By 1934 he had been renamed Goofy and become part of the regular gang of Disney characters. Although he featured in his own series of short films from the 1940s to the 1960s, however, it was not until the 1990s that Goofy got his own TV series, *Goof Troop*, which included a selection of dedicated regular characters and which led to his appearance in two feature-length films: *A Goofy Movie* (1995) and *An Extremely Goofy Movie* (2000). He continues to make guest appearances in Mickey Mouse TV shows.

CANINE RULES OF HIERARCHY

If you keep more than one dog at home, it is important to remember not to treat them as equal in status at all times. The owner or handler has to take the place of the pack leader, and each dog by instinct and social learning knows its place in the rank order of subordination to the leader. To treat dogs equally could therefore cause dissension and even make the dogs slightly less certain of your role as the pack leader.

CAIRN TERRIER / BULLDOG CROSSBREEDS

Each has 3 named crossbreeds:

an American bulldog &
a Boxer = a Bulloxer
a Bull terrier = a Bulldog terrier
a Pekingese = a Bullnese

a Cairn terrier &
a Shih Tzu = a Care-Tzu
a West Highland terrier = a Cairland terrier
a Yorkshire terrier = a Carkie

THE DOG AS BACK SEAT DRIVER

"Dogs feel very strongly that they should always go
with you in the car, in case the need should arise for them
to bark violently at nothing right in your ear."

DAVE BARRY (B. 1947) *U.S. author and humorous columnist*

WEREWOLVES & LYCANTHROPY

Stories in which a person—generally a man—temporarily transforms completely or partially into a wolf have been current since ancient Greek and Roman times, and generally also include elements of serial murder, mutilation, and/or cannibalism. In reality it is these acts, committed by-humans, that until the last decades of the nineteenth century in much of Europe were generally responsible for the stories. For residents local to such events, when they were revealed in horrific detail, it was preferable to think that they had been carried out by a wolf rather than by a neighbor. (Alternatively, the neighbor might be said in mitigation to have been bewitched, cursed by a third party, or to have been affected by a full moon.)

At the same time, there is today a recognized form of psychosis in which a person truly believes he or she is being transformed, has been transformed, or is sometimes transformed into a wolf. Clinical lycanthropy (ancient Greek *lyk-* "wolf", *anthrōp-* "man") of this kind is rare—rare enough for the meaning of the term in North America and some other English-speaking areas to have been extended so that the basis of the psychotic delusion may be an animal other than a wolf.

WHY "CAVALIER KING CHARLES SPANIEL"?

The King Charles spaniel—which is also known as the English toy spaniel—is so called because it was a great favorite of King Charles II after his restoration to the British throne in 1660. He is said to have personally exercised his dogs in St. James's Park, London, regularly.

King Charles spaniels today are actually larger than they were in the seventeenth century. The Cavalier King Charles spaniel is slightly larger and heavier still—it is sometimes described as the largest breed of all the toy dogs—and it also has a longer nose.

As a "younger" form of the King Charles spaniel (it was first bred only during the initial decades of the twentieth century), this breed was given the description of "Cavalier" because that description could also apply to the younger King Charles from the time of the English Civil War (1642–1651, against the "Roundheads" of Oliver Cromwell) to his restoration.

RECOMMENDED BOWL HEIGHTS

Manufacturers of water bowls for dogs make them in various sizes, intended for the different sizes of dog. Too few owners realize, however, that a water bowl should be positioned also at a height above the ground that accords with the size of the dog—not even a very short-legged dog should have to slurp up water from ground level. Or so the manufacturers say—and they have produced tables of preferred height maximums in order to promote the theory.

SIZE OF DOG	BOWL CAPACITY	BOWL DIAMETER	MAX. BRIM HEIGHT
Small *Chihuahua to Yorkshire terrier*	2 cups 475 ml 1 u.s./0.83 u.k. pint	6½ in 16.5 cm	10 in 25.4 cm
Medium *Beagle* to *Whippet*	4 cups 950 ml 2 u.s./1.66 u.k. pints	8 in 20 cm	13¾ in 35 cm
Large *Afghan hound to Golden retriever*	8 cups 1.9 liters 4 u.s./3.6 u.k. pints	9¾ in 24.75 cm	19⅓ in 49 cm
Extra large *Great Dane to Newfoundland*	12 cups 2.8 liters 6 u.s./5 u.k. pints	11 in 28 cm	24½ in 62.2 cm

TITIAN & DOGS

Tiziano Vecelli (*c.* 1488–1576), in English known as Titian, was the leader of the sixteenth-century Venetian school of Renaissance art. He included dogs in a number of his portraits of contemporary aristocrats and courtesans, generally in such a way as to suggest a comment on the character of the primary object of the portrait. The pet dogs shown with nude courtesans, for example, may represent a contrast between fidelity and insincerity, or may even correspond to a suggestion of sexual profligacy or deviance.

———— GAUEKO, BASQUE DOG OF DARKNESS ————

Gaueko ("[He] of the night" in the Basque language) is the spirit of darkness and the dangers for humans that darkness encompasses, including fear of violent death. He takes the form of a large wolfhound that sometimes walks upright, eats whole flocks of sheep (and occasionally their shepherds too), and howls in the distance on the blackest nights of winter. It is Gaueko who warns a man silly enough to be out alone on a dark night to go home at once and stay indoors until the friendly sun rises. And it is Gaueko who, if this man is foolish enough to ignore his warning, ensures that such intemperate defiance does not go unpunished.

———— ANCIENT HERITAGE OF THE SALUKI ————

The elegant Saluki may well be the first major type of dog deliberately bred by humans: they were apparently being bred in Mesopotamia in 3,000 BCE . . . although this is also said of the greyhound. Images of dogs that look remarkably similar to Salukis have additionally been discovered on Egyptian tombs dating from a similar period.

———— CANINE PHYSIQUE & SWIMMING ABILITY ————

The Newfoundland has webbed feet and a highly water-resistant coat: it can accordingly swim extremely well. The basset hound has short, stumpy legs and very heavy bones: it cannot swim at all.

———— PRAIRIE DU CHIEN, WISCONSIN ————

The county seat of Crawford County, Wisconsin—Prairie du Chien—is often described as Wisconsin's second oldest city. It was founded in the late seventeenth century by French explorers and fur trappers, who seem to have given the local area, including the settlement, its name partly because the inhabitants of the place when they arrived were mainly Fox Indians, and partly because the contemporary chief of those Native Americans was himself named Alim, which translates as "The Dog" (French *Le Chien*). The resident population in 2000 stood at just over 6,000, but this number is massively swollen in the summer season by tourists who come to see the city's 5 National Historic Landmarks and its 9 sites on the National Register of Historic Places. It is also the location for an annual Prairie Dog Blues Festival featuring blues bands from all over the world (although "prairie dog" is of course not a translation of Prairie du Chien).

PROSTATE PROBLEMS IN MEN & DOGS

Male humans and male dogs are the only animals that have prostate glands. As they reach beyond middle age, the prostate is more likely to cause serious health problems. A man may suffer from malignant cancer of the prostate, which causes constriction of the urethra and difficulty and pain on urination. In a dog, the prostate may also cause constriction by swelling against adjoining organs, but the growth is usually caused not so much by cancer as by ageing (or occasionally by bacterial infection), and the main constricted organ is the rectum. The dog therefore has difficulty and pain on defecation. This is the most common cause of constipation and excretory straining in male dogs.

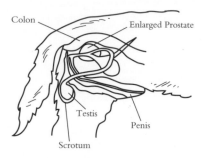

Colon — Enlarged Prostate

Testis

Penis

Scrotum

A dog with a painful prostate walks abnormally, taking short steps with hind legs that are rigidly straight. Surgery may ease or correct the condition, but in any case the condition is far less potentially life-threatening in a dog than it is in a man.

PRESIDENT JOHNSON'S BEAGLES

Lyndon B. Johnson, president of the United States 1963–1969, had two beagles: one male and one female. They were named Him and Her.

RESERVOIR DOGS

Reservoir Dogs was the debut feature film written and directed by Quentin Tarantino and starring Harvey Keitel. Released in 1992, it quickly became a cult hit because of its casual violence and its profane dialogue with allusions to pop culture. A video game based on the failed-heist story was issued in 2006.

──────── WILL EAT ANYTHING; LOVES CHILDREN ────────

Children under the age of 10 should *never* be left unsupervised with *any* dog, even for a few moments.

──────── CIRCLING BEFORE TOUCHDOWN ────────

Dogs (and cats) tend to walk around in a circle two or 3 times before they lie down. This is because in the wild—in savanna grassland or amid bracken and succulent shoots on a forest floor—this circling movement compresses and flattens foliage into a more comfortable surface, discourages insects, and ensures that there is a means of instant escape in more than one direction in an emergency. Many dog beds commercially available today are accordingly made circular in shape.

──────── THE DOG AS OPTIMIST ────────

"The dog has an enviable mind; it remembers the nice
things in life and quickly blots out the nasty."
BARBARA WOODHOUSE (1910–1988) *Irish author and dog trainer*

──────── SILENT HUNTER: THE BASENJI ────────

The Basenji does not bark: it can growl, snuffle, or whine—but not bark— although it can make a strange yodeling sort of sound. It is also rather strange to look at, but it has an ancient history as a pet. Basenji were used as hunting dogs in Africa as early as in the third millennium BCE, prized for their intelligence, their keen sense of smell, and their silence when hunting.

──────── ARGOS, FAITHFUL DOG OF ODYSSEUS ────────

According to ancient Greek author Homer, Argos was the dog who, when the hero Odysseus finally arrived home in Ithaca having left 20 years earlier for the Trojan War, was the only one of the household to recognize him although Odysseus was in disguise. And having recognized him, the dog died content. It may have been that act of recognition that gave him his name, however, for *argos* can mean "with clear eyes." It can alternatively mean "clear to the eyes" and therefore "white"—which might again explain the name if the dog was intended to be of that color.